Jeffrey A. Brown

COGNITIVE
WRITING

Leading The Way

Collection One

Cognitive Writing

Leading The Way

Jeffrey A. Brown

Self Published

Cognitive Writing — Leading The Way

ISBN 979-8-9937679-0-1 (Paperback)
ISBN 979-8-9937679-1-8 (Hardcover)

Contents

Introduction

For one year, I published two leadership insights per week on LinkedIn. What started as a personal commitment became a conversation with over 55,000 professionals navigating similar challenges.

This collection brings together 58 of those insights, organized to take you from foundational principles to advanced leadership strategies. Each post stands alone—read straight through or jump to what is relevant for you today.

Written with Cognitive Writing™—simple language conveying complex ideas, creating space for you to discover meaning from your own perspective. These are lessons from the trenches, tested in real organizations, delivered with clarity.

"If you can't explain it simply, you don't understand it well enough."

Connect with me on LinkedIn: linkedin.com/in/jeffrey-a-brown

Welcome to Leading The Way.

Section 1

The Foundation

Start here: What leadership is all about

Redefining Leadership: What It Truly Means to Lead

Every role in a successful team is important—there are no minor roles. Imagine a high-tech engine: if you remove even its smallest component, the whole system could fail. This is true for teams too. Success is impossible without everyone's unique contributions.

As an Executive, I often talk with team members who tell me my role is more important than theirs. I emphasize that their hard work is what enables me to do my job effectively. Our roles are different but equally important.

Teams are often represented as an organizational chart, with leaders at the top. However, real leadership isn't about being above others; it's about being one with the team. I make it a point to sit among my team members during meetings, not at the head of the table. I do this intentionally to show them that no role is too small, and no task too insignificant. It takes collaboration to achieve our goals.

Leadership as a Two-Way Street

Effective leadership means being humble and removing obstacles so your team can succeed. It's about understanding that each team member plays a role in the team's success. This involves actively listening to and supporting each individual's diverse contributions.

Transparency is Key

As leaders, we must provide clear expectations with open communication. Without this clarity, team members may feel lost or even frustrated, not knowing how to perform at their best. Remember, good leadership is about balance: we must give as much as we get. In your next meeting, consider asking, "What can I do to support you?" This question demonstrates your commitment to transparency and reinforces your dedication to empowering the team.

Take Action: Engage and Reflect

Take a moment to think about how you could demonstrate appreciation for each member of the team. Could you do more to enhance transparency, set better expectations, and foster better communication? Start by sharing your thoughts on why and how you make decisions, actively seeking input from each team member, and openly acknowledging everyone's wins, even the little ones. Let's redefine leadership together, one inclusive and supportive step at a time.

Lead with Authenticity: Unlock the Power of Trust

Authenticity begins with self-awareness. It means being yourself and knowing who you are. When you're authentic, you make it easy for your team to connect with you and talk openly.

Authenticity is also about self-acceptance. It's about building resilience and confidence. This helps you understand not just your own feelings but also how others might feel. Embracing who you are fosters empathy, making room for everyone's differences and creating an inclusive workplace that celebrates diversity.

Authenticity is about being trustworthy. It means being honest and always doing the right thing. Trust works both ways and when you lead with authenticity you build a team that believes in each other. Your honest approach sets the tone for a dependable and trustworthy environment.

Authenticity lets you lead by example and reflect the values you believe in. Your team watches what you do and learns from you, becoming a reflection of your leadership style. When you're true to yourself, it inspires others to be their best. So, being yourself not only makes you a good leader but also inspires your team to be the best they can be.

Authenticity is about self-awareness, self-acceptance, empathy, honesty, and integrity — these are all keys to higher Emotional Intelligence. Let authenticity become your superpower, making you a great leader and paving the way for your team's success.

Being a Leader Starts with Being Human

As a leadership mentor, one of the most common rookie mistakes I see is the belief that respect comes from knowing everything. New leaders often feel they need to project confidence by acting as though they have all the answers, fearing that admitting uncertainty or making a mistake might undermine their authority. Ironically, this approach often backfires.

The truth is, the best leaders don't need to be perfect—they need to be human.

Leadership Begins with Humanity

The first step to great leadership is simple: be yourself. You were chosen for your role because of your experience and abilities, not because you know everything. You've got nothing to prove. By showing up authentically—flaws and all—you make it easier for your team to trust you.

Instead of standing above your team, stand beside them. When you collaborate, show vulnerability, and stay open, you signal that you're there to work with them, not just oversee them. A leader who admits mistakes and seeks input creates a space where people feel safe taking risks, learning, and growing.

Rethink the Org Chart

Organizational charts are often misunderstood. Too many people see them as rigid hierarchies—a top-down chain of command that separates leaders from their teams. The most effective organizations are flat in spirit, even if not in structure. They work more like a team, where success depends on everyone doing their part and working together toward a shared goal.

Like any good team, people rely on one another and succeed—or fail—together. Every role matters, and no one achieves success alone.

Building Trust Through Authenticity

Over the years, I've led many teams and continue to bring a wealth of experience to my role as a Fractional Executive. Yet, I've had people tell me they find me intimidating. This feedback always gives me pause, because I've always focused on building connections over titles or trying to seem perfect.

I welcome mistakes and value those moments when I can ask, *"Tell me more."* For me, leadership isn't about projecting authority—it's about creating a space where curiosity thrives and ideas can take shape.

When you let go of the need to have all the answers, you create space for your team to share their perspectives. Openness leads to collaboration, and collaboration builds trust. Over time, that trust empowers your team to challenge assumptions, pitch ideas, and grow individually while contributing to something greater.

The Power of Unknown

At its core, leadership isn't about knowing everything—it's about building a place where learning and growth thrive. Saying *"I don't know"* isn't a weakness; it's an invitation. It creates a culture of curiosity, humbleness, and openness to learn for your team.

Great leaders don't try to be perfect—they just strive to be real. And that's what I believe it means to be human—to be a leader. What do you believe?

Leading Without Ego: A Guide for Humble Leadership

Why are you afraid to ask questions or to look foolish? Why didn't you notice that a team member wasn't performing at their best, and why didn't you step in to help? These are the questions that may signal your ego is getting in the way. Even the best leaders can struggle with these real-world challenges.

Self-awareness and self-acceptance remain the cornerstone of ego-free leadership. It's about understanding yourself, recognizing your strengths, acknowledging areas for growth, and accepting who you are. In my own leadership journey, I've discovered that focusing on self-awareness has been a game-changer both at work and in my personal life. Being self-aware and accepting who I am has given me the confidence to lead authentically and build a trust-based culture within my teams.

Leadership is not about perfection; it's about embracing those imperfections and learning from them. Acknowledging mistakes and seeking improvement are signs of good leadership. As a leader, being comfortable looking foolish and asking honest questions fosters an environment where team members feel encouraged to do the same. Don't believe that by asking questions the team may think you are not a good and experienced leader; instead, know that they will respect you more as a human as well as a leader. Remember, if you don't ask, you won't know the answer next time.

Shifting the focus from you to the individuals on your team is transformative. Recognizing and addressing the needs of team members allows you to work collaboratively to improve both individuals and the team as a whole. By avoiding self-absorption, leaders can spot those who need help and guidance, ultimately lifting them up and contributing to the overall team's success. Measure your success only by the success of your team.

The most important leadership skill may also be the hardest to learn. Building a foundation for ego-free leadership involves honest self-awareness, self-acceptance, and a servant-leader mentality. It's an ongoing journey of learning, evolving, honesty, and transparently putting others' needs before your own. Encouraging this mindset within yourself will bring continuous improvement and empower you to a whole new level of leading successful teams without the hindrance of unchecked egos.

A Fresh Perspective: Servant Leadership in the Classroom

In my journey as an executive, I've witnessed firsthand the power of servant leadership. Imagine a workplace where every voice is valued, every individual feels empowered, and diversity thrives. This is not simply an idea; it's a practical model that extends its influence beyond office walls, enhancing work-life balance, productivity, and societal well-being. Leaders who embrace this style prioritize empathy, understanding, and diversity, creating environments where individuals can flourish. Through their emotional intelligence and genuine integrity, servant leaders are paving the way for a future where empathy and diversity are celebrated and everyone has the opportunity to thrive. Yet, a critical question comes to mind: when and where should leaders begin to learn these invaluable skills?

The answer: infuse these principles into a younger arena—the classroom. Imagine if elementary school teachers incorporated leadership mentoring into their daily interactions with students, emphasizing service, diversity, and collaboration as core principles of learning. Such an approach could transform typical classroom dynamics, making every group activity a lesson in leadership and every project an exercise in teamwork and mutual respect. After all, children spend a significant portion of their formative years in school, making teachers their daily role models.

Traditional leadership has too long been associated with control, ego, money, power, and title, but what if we redefined it? What if our students were guided by teachers who exemplify servant leadership, where celebrating collaborative achievements, nurturing individual strengths, and fostering an inclusive environment was the norm? This educational shift could cultivate a generation of leaders who value empathy, integrity, and diversity.

By nurturing leadership skills in young students, we enhance their academic experience and prepare them to be compassionate, forward-thinking leaders who drive positive change in their communities and beyond. This effort transcends mere educational enrichment—a strategic investment in molding a workforce ready and equipped to excel in leadership roles. Envision a classroom that functions as a mini-society, where teachers act as mentors, and every lesson serves as a stepping stone toward building tomorrow's servant leaders.

Equip our educators with the necessary tools and resources to bring leadership skills to students. I urge educational policymakers, school administrators, and community leaders to invest in professional development programs focused on mentorship and collaborative teaching methods. When we empower teachers as leaders, the potential for our collective future knows no bounds. This vision—one that highlights the pivotal role teachers play in shaping not just young minds but entire societies—is within our reach. Together, we can make it a reality.

From Transactions to Trust: Building Lasting Partnerships

Do you want to unlock the secret to winning in today's evolving world of sales? Perhaps the key is hidden in not focusing on the transaction at all.

In the competitive world of sales and marketing, let's reconsider our age-old, number-driven strategies. Faced with a younger generation that places more stock on value and trust, the time to pivot is now. Instead of focusing solely on meeting quotas and rushing to close deals, let's shift our efforts towards a more meaningful strategy – mastering the art of building genuine partnerships founded in trust. Having witnessed firsthand the transformative power of this approach, I can attest to its effectiveness.

Consider this: customers aren't just making a transaction; they're investing in a partnership. It goes beyond the immediate service to encompass the company's overall mission and vision. Trust has become the indispensable currency driving successful deals. I've fallen victim to the challenges imposed by frequent rotations of sales reps, thereby hindering their ability to truly understand their customers' needs—my needs. Allowing reps to build long-term relationships with clients can lead to more sustainable success.

Now, let's explore some practical steps to cultivate these lasting relationships. Effective leadership involves actively listening to your sales teams and customers. Instead of imposing changes from above, start by asking, *"What do you need to be successful in your role?"* This shift fosters a collaborative environment where trust can naturally thrive.

Constructing enduring relationships is a marathon, not a sprint. Frequent rotations of sales reps impede their ability to truly understand your customer's business and anticipate their needs at the right time. In today's world of sales and marketing, patience isn't just a virtue; it's a strategic advantage.

To all Sales Executives and team managers, my humble suggestion is to embrace this paradigm shift. Prioritize consciously building relationships based on trust, and you're likely to observe a remarkable improvement in overall success. Keep in mind, that in a world where transactions follow trust, a change in perspective can act as the catalyst for unparalleled growth.

Whether you are in Sales or working with clients, think about how shifting from transactions to authentic partnerships could transform your business. If you or your organization has already embraced this strategy, consider the impact it has had on your success.

The Immeasurable Value of Good Leadership

Behind every successful team is an outstanding leader. The significance of effective leadership won't be measurable using standard metrics like KPIs or KRAs. In a recent discussion with a colleague, I reflected on the transformation of a senior team member. This individual began to take ownership and demonstrate a genuine passion for the product. When asked, *"What changed?"* the answer was simple: **leadership.** By trusting them and showing what we could achieve together, they became inspired and empowered him to do more. This shift underscores the profound impact good leadership can have.

Trust

With a competent leader, a team develops a sense of psychological safety. Employees who feel trusted and valued go above and beyond in their efforts. When expectations are clear and leadership is transparent and trusting, teams don't just meet expectations—they exceed them. It's remarkable what happens when team members feel supported by their leader.

Empowerment

It's not always about increasing the team size; it's about empowering the people you already have. Leading with openness and fostering a strong buy-in for the vision encourages team members to work harder and strive to prove their capabilities to both themselves and their leader.

Value

There will always be jobs that offer higher pay elsewhere. However, the feeling of being valued and making a meaningful difference often outweighs any paycheck with an employee number. A disengaged team will not be motivated by salary alone. In contrast, an average team, when effectively motivated and led, can achieve exceptional results.

Vision

A good leader understands the importance of guiding individuals rather than merely managing teams. They recognize that appreciating each team member's unique needs and priorities empowers individuals, thereby enhancing their contributions to the team's overall success. This approach requires personalized guidance, emotional intelligence, diversity, and collaboration. It's not about pushing the team harder but about nurturing each individual's potential, which in turn drives the team to achieve great results.

Look around—if you are fortunate enough to have a strong leader, do everything you can to retain them. After all, can you afford to lose such a valuable asset from your team?

The Power of Intentional Leadership

As a leadership mentor, my clients often discuss the challenges they face with various projects and initiatives. One of the first things I do is reframe our conversation with a simple yet profound question: *"What is your why?"* My goal is to get them to think about the reasons driving their actions.

Every day, leadership is filled with decisions, ranging from which projects to prioritize to how best to allocate resources and manage team dynamics. One key factor that separates effective leaders from the rest: *intentionality.*

Leading with Purpose

When you lead with intention, the effects are both immediate and extensive. Leaders who embrace this approach enhance their productivity and sharpen their decision-making abilities, enabling them to stay focused on their goals. This mindset of intentionality, mirrored across the team, fosters efficiency, cohesion, and motivation. A clear understanding of the *"why"* helps align the team and gives transparency to the value of their efforts, driving their engagement.

What Does It Mean to Lead with Intention?

Intentional leadership involves being mindful and deliberate in every action. It's not just about reacting to situations or going through the motions; it's about understanding the reasons behind every decision and aligning those decisions with your core values, objectives, and the mission of the company. This thoughtful approach prevents missteps and ensures that every choice propels you toward your long-term goals.

Interestingly, sometimes the best action is inaction. Intentional leaders recognize moments when the most effective strategy is to do nothing. This isn't due to indecision or lack of direction but should be a strategic decision leading to the best possible outcome.

Unlocking Potential Through Intentionality

Embracing intentional leadership unlocks your full potential and inspires those around you to reach their own. The far-reaching benefits of this leadership style extend well beyond immediate project outcomes; it fosters employee satisfaction and cultivates a positive culture within your organization. Consistently aligning your actions with your goals creates a workplace environment that is built on trust and thrives on transparency and intention.

So the next time you feel like you're just going through the motions or faced with a tough decision, pause to ask yourself *"why."* Welcome this moment of reflection which can lead to successful outcomes for yourself and your entire team. Consider incorporating time to reflect on your decisions into your daily routine to ensure they align with your intentions. This practice can transform your leadership style into a dynamic force that propels both professional growth and team achievements to new heights.

Section 2

Building Your Team

The people: hiring, empowering, developing

The Humanity of Hiring Great People

In an age where technology touches every corner of our lives, many companies have shifted to hiring through automated talent acquisition systems (ATS) and AI-driven analytics. These tools promise efficiency, helping hiring managers quickly scan for skills they think will ensure success in a role.

But do they truly help you find the right people?

Focus on Potential

Resumes focus on hard skills, listing qualifications, and searching for keywords to match a role's requirements. Yet, when a candidate's capabilities don't check all the boxes, these systems can miss true potential. This approach may screen out individuals who could bring the fresh ideas and diverse perspectives your team needs.

Have a Conversation

In my work, I do a lot of *"connection calls."* In about 30 to 45 minutes, I can often tell if this is someone I'd want to work with. Have a real conversation with the candidate—evaluate whether they would thrive within your team's culture and if they're highly motivated to contribute to your team's success. It comes down to going back to basics: listening, engaging, and being present. While technology may bring efficiency, it can't replace the depth of human insight.

Close the Deal

The modern interview process often drags on for weeks, even months, as companies feel compelled to evaluate every potential candidate before making an offer. But waiting too long risks losing top talent to other opportunities. When you find a candidate who's an ideal match for both the role and your team's culture—make the offer! Yes, there may always be a *"better"* candidate out there, but extending the process only increases the risk of losing the perfect one right in front of you.

Back to Basics

I urge hiring teams to bring a human-centered approach back to the process. Yes, it may mean putting in the time to read resumes and have real conversations with candidates. In a world where anyone can hire a resume writer, does that piece of paper really tell you about the person?

Refine your hiring process:
• Look for Commitment: A history of staying with previous companies often signals reliability and dedication.
• Recognize Growth: Promotions over time indicate hard work, progression, and readiness to take on more responsibility.
• Observe Career Progression: Multiple short stints can suggest a candidate is still searching for direction. Seek individuals whose career moves demonstrate strategic growth.

These qualities are challenging for resume-scanning software to capture. Automated systems might work for filling seats, but if your goal is to find high achievers and career employees who will elevate your organization, focus on more than the checkboxes.

Hiring isn't just about finding skills—it's about finding people who will strengthen the culture you've built. This effort starts with HR. Let's not lose sight of the *"human"* in Human Resources. My ask is simple: *Hire people, not resumes.*

The Art of Interviewing: Strategies for Attracting Top Talent

As a mentor and fractional tech executive, I have conducted numerous interviews, and candidates often express gratitude, having gained insights from our discussion. This feedback highlights the mutual learning that occurs during an effective interview process, enriching both parties and setting the stage for ongoing professional development.

Prepare for the interview

Begin by preparing a set of well-thought-out questions and use this same set for each candidate to simplify comparisons. Additionally, note down the answers you anticipate to help keep the interview focused and on track.

Start with an easy one

A good place to start any interview is to ask candidates about themselves outside of the professional environment. You can respond in kind. After all, you are hiring people—get to know who they are.

Describe the position

Another initial question is to ask candidates to describe the position they are interviewing for. This helps ensure their understanding aligns with the company's. Establishing clear expectations from the start is essential for successful alignment.

Look for Mindfulness

Instead of focusing solely on their existing knowledge (already in their resume), ask questions that provide insight into their thought processes and how they handle real-world scenarios.

Show Your Commitment to Growth

If a candidate answers incorrectly, offer a second chance and, if needed, the correct answer. This demonstrates your commitment to a learning environment and clearly shows your ability to provide mentorship. After all, isn't this what you would do for an existing employee?

Ask the impossible

Ask an impossible question to gauge problem-solving skills and adaptability. It's more about the attempt than the answer and allows you to assess resilience and creativity. How quickly will they give up when the going gets tough?

Encourage Honesty

Candidates who seek clarification showcase their thoughtfulness and eagerness to understand. Introducing a question that prompts an *"I don't know"* response assesses their honesty and lack of ego. The last thing you want is a *"know it all."*

At the end of the interview, leave a moment to verbally summarize your observations, providing an opportunity to correct any misconceptions or misunderstandings. Giving immediate feedback creates a lasting impression of your leadership style.

Tip: Always stay mindful of HR guidelines to ensure the appropriateness of your interview questions.

Keep in mind, that candidates are evaluating you and your company just as much as you're assessing them. They may be exploring opportunities with multiple organizations, so making a positive impression is essential. Be approachable, demonstrate your supportiveness, and convey that you're someone they can learn from to advance their career. This approach is a great way to leave a positive lasting impression of your company.

Beyond the Screening: Strategic Interviewing

Many executives have excelled in long-standing roles, advancing through the ranks and building successful careers. They've likely hired countless professionals and mastered the art of interviewing to attract top talent. Yet, when it's their turn to enter the job market, they often find themselves unprepared for the modern interview process.

I work with executives and leaders who are transitioning into new roles, coaching them on how to pitch themselves effectively and secure that next opportunity.

The Right Strategy

In today's hiring process, you'll likely speak with an HR representative, a hiring manager, and possibly an executive. Each of these interviews requires a different strategy, as each interviewer is focused on a specific goal.

The Screening

During an HR screening, your objective is to demonstrate your qualifications and make it clear that you're an ideal fit. Since HR may not be deeply familiar with your specific area of expertise, it's up to you to bridge that gap, helping them easily check off the boxes that align your experience with the role without going into too much detail.

Strategically navigating this initial screening is key. Here's how you can authentically frame your skills to match HR's checklist without selling yourself short. The goal is to make it simple for HR to recognize your capabilities and move you forward to more in-depth conversations that will truly showcase your expertise.

Successful Reframes for Key Skills:

• **Data Analysis**
Question: *"Do you have experience with data analytics?"*
Truth: *"I've never worked as a data analyst."*
Strategic reframe: *"Yes, I've tracked sales trends and used data analytics extensively to summarize financial data."*

• **Project Management**
Question: "Have you managed large-scale projects?"
Truth: "I've never held a project manager title."
Strategic reframe: *"Yes, I've coordinated complex initiatives involving multiple stakeholders. In my previous role, I managed intricate projects involving timelines, budgets, and cross-functional team collaboration."*

• **Financial Planning**
Question: *"Do you have experience with budgeting and forecasting?"*
Truth: *"I've never worked in finance."*
Strategic reframe: *"Yes, I've managed large budgets and regularly applied data analytics for accurate forecasting."*

These responses position you as a well-rounded candidate, helping you move through the initial screening phase and into conversations that allow for a deeper dive into your unique qualifications. This strategic approach is particularly valuable for candidates with broad skill sets or unconventional backgrounds.

Leadership from Above: Empowerment by Letting Go

As someone who often mentors new leaders, I frequently encounter a misconception about the essence of leadership. They mistakenly equate leadership with authority and control, believing that once they ascend to a leadership role, they must dictate every aspect of their team's actions—which leads to micromanagement. However, the heart of good leadership actually lies in surrendering control rather than asserting it.

Imagine leadership as a bustling city block, with each floor of a building symbolizing a different stage in your journey as a leader. At ground level, as an individual contributor, you're in the thick of it, hands-on and immersed in the action. But as you climb the corporate ladder, you ascend to higher floors, gaining a broader perspective but relinquishing direct control.

Starting as a manager, you're like a resident peering out from a second-story window, able to see more of the block but unable to intervene as directly. Further up, as a director or VP, you're on the skyscraper's upper floors, with an even wider view but less ability to influence what's happening on the ground.

True leadership isn't about asserting power; it's about empowering others. It's about using your elevated vantage point to support and guide your team, not dictate their every move. Being a servant leader means prioritizing your team's success above your own ego, and that includes fostering their independence. The ultimate goal? make your team so self-sufficient that they no longer need your constant oversight, freeing you to tackle new challenges and continue growing as a leader.

So, to all the new leaders out there: remember, leadership isn't about control—it's about letting go. Embrace the view from above, support your team until they can navigate the streets on their own, and prepare yourself for the next ascent.

Team Management: Practical Tips for Building an Effective Team

Looking to build a great team? As a mentor and fractional tech executive, here are strategies that have proven effective for me:

Job Descriptions: Write your own! Crafting the perfect job description that matches your team's specific needs is essential. This step attracts the right candidates and sets clear expectations, ensuring that everyone knows exactly what the role entails.

Internships: Embrace internships! They offer a dual benefit: you contribute to the community and enhance your company's reputation. Think of it as an extended interview process, allowing you to observe potential employees in real work situations. Interns who transition to full-time roles often bring loyalty and a deep understanding of your company's culture, having grown alongside the business.

Experience Levels: Hiring people with 3 to 5 years of experience often hits the sweet spot. They adapt quickly, which allows them to grow and thrive within your team. When seeking more seasoned professionals for roles that demand deep expertise, be prepared for a longer hiring process, potentially taking 6 to 9 months. Patience in these situations often pays off.

Diversity: Building a team with diverse backgrounds enriches the workplace culturally and intellectually. A varied team brings different perspectives that enhance creativity and drive innovation, leading to more effective problem-solving and a more inclusive work environment.

Education and Job History: Value candidates who have earned a degree, as this demonstrates their dedication to completing a long-term goal. Whether the degree is from a related field of study is less important than the commitment shown in achieving this milestone. Also, consider candidates who have stayed with a previous employer for at least three years, as this indicates their ability to commit and suggests they are likely to provide long-term stability to your team.

Senior Members: Retain seasoned professionals on your team. They set higher standards and provide mentorship, enhancing the overall quality and raising the bar for the entire group.

Let Them Hire: Empower your senior team members to lead the hiring process for positions below their level. This approach promotes responsibility and helps ensure new hires integrate well with the existing team dynamics.

Referrals: Never underestimate the power of referrals. They are one of the best ways to find individuals who will integrate seamlessly into your team. A strong referral culture also indicates a healthy work environment, as employees are confident enough to recommend the company to their peers.

Culture Fit: Lastly, ensure that new hires are a good match for your team's culture. The right person in the right environment will thrive, while a mismatch can disrupt team dynamics.

By choosing the right individuals you can build a team, ready to achieve anything they set their minds to.

A Strategic Decision: Promoting Your Top Performers

Should You Promote Your Top Individual Contributors to Leadership Positions?

Promoting your top individual contributors to leadership positions seems like a straightforward recognition of their hard work, but is it always the right move? A top contributor excels at tasks and projects, often being highly efficient, goal-oriented, and a subject matter expert. They are adept at problem-solving, making independent decisions, and delivering results. These individuals thrive on being hands-on and are often recognized for their expertise and ability to deliver high-quality work.

In contrast, transitioning to a leadership role requires a shift in focus from individual achievements to guiding and supporting others. Effective leaders prioritize team success over personal accomplishments and must be willing to delegate tasks, provide mentorship, and empower team members to succeed. This transition from *"doing"* to *"enabling others to do"* can be challenging for individuals accustomed to focusing solely on their own work. Good leaders possess strong interpersonal skills, emotional intelligence, and the ability to navigate complex team dynamics. They inspire trust, communicate effectively, and resolve conflicts while maintaining a clear vision and direction for the team.

It's rare to find someone who naturally excels both as a top performer and as a leader. The decision to promote a top individual contributor should be made after careful consideration of its impact on the team's overall performance. Promoting your top performer could potentially disrupt the team's dynamic and negatively affect its productivity, raising the question: Would you intentionally sideline your star player?

Without advancing them to leadership roles, what are effective ways to acknowledge your top performers? Consider promoting them within their current roles, moving them to a Senior or higher level appropriate for their field. This gives them the recognition they deserve while inspiring others on the team to look up to them and strive to emulate their success. Another effective strategy is to consider increasing their salary. Gone are the days when leaders must be the highest-paid members of the team. Highly skilled individual contributors should be well compensated for their expertise and unique skills. After all, ask yourself which is harder to replace: a good leader or a subject matter expert with years of tribal knowledge for your product.

Leading a Successful Team: Understanding the Engineering Mind

Leading a successful engineering team involves understanding and applying principles that inspire and fuel the engineer. The engineering mind is inherently curious and creative, relentlessly driven by the desire to understand and solve problems. The following outlines a simple yet powerful set of leadership principles that, when applied effectively, can ignite such a mindset and lead to remarkable success.

Lead by Example

Set the standard for your team. Teams often mirror the behavior of their leaders. Demonstrating tireless dedication fosters mutual respect and effort.

Clarity

Engineers thrive on well-defined problems, and the nature of a challenge ignites their passion for finding solutions. With a clearly understood problem, they gain the motivation to engage. Clarity also means establishing a well-defined scope and ensuring it remains consistent throughout a project, thereby sharpening focus and efficiently directing efforts.

Efficiency

Renowned for their dedication to solving problems, engineers have little tolerance for wasteful practices. Establishing efficient and sensible processes is essential for their success. In software engineering, efficiency means that every investment of time and energy must yield tangible outcomes, like how every line of code should contribute to functional, released software.

Trust

Just as you would trust a skilled plumber with your home, you must trust software engineers with your code. Software Developers spend years honing their skills to master their craft. Often, leaders who oversee teams of engineers may not have a technical background. It is, therefore, essential to extend deserved trust and let their expertise lead the way. The results can be truly astounding.

Trust but Verify

Trusting your team is essential for success, yet blind trust can lead to unforeseen challenges. Measure their progress and hold them accountable using clear metrics that demonstrate efficiency. Effective leadership requires a balance between trust and oversight—what is measured can be managed and improved. Aim to maintain a high level of quality, fostering transparency while avoiding micromanagement.

Value

Above all, engineers need to feel valued. Treating them well, showing genuine care, and celebrating wins—even the small ones—ensures they know their contributions are appreciated.

Transformational Leadership

This is a simple recipe for building a highly efficient and successful engineering team. However, remember that *"simple"* does not mean *"easy."* Achieving success requires time, dedication, and commitment.

Reflect on your leadership style: *Which principles are you excelling at, and where could you use some improvement?*

Mentorship: Shaping Leaders for Success

Recently, a young leader asked me, *"How important is mentorship in shaping a leader?"* This question sparked a reflection on my own experiences and the pivotal role mentorship has played in my development.

Throughout my career, I've learned from exceptional leaders, drawing wisdom from their wins and learning valuable lessons from their missteps. While I have never had a formal mentor, I've come to understand the profound impact of mentorship as I now find myself guiding others.

Experience Sharing

A mentor's rich experience offers insights far beyond any textbook. Their personal stories, interwoven with successes and setbacks, provide practical and memorable lessons. Great mentors are seasoned professionals and adept storytellers, leaving lasting impressions that ring true throughout one's career.

Accelerated Learning Curve

Mentors guide you along your journey, challenging your assumptions and encouraging you to step out of your comfort zone. This fosters rapid growth and helps you manage your expectations, ensuring progression at a sustainable pace.

Ongoing Support

Good mentors help you celebrate your victories, no matter how small, keeping you and your team motivated. They stand by you during tough times, helping you rise up, dust off, and tackle new challenges. They offer a fresh perspective on failures, reframing them into valuable lessons that shape future endeavors.

Potential Pitfalls

It's important to recognize the potential downsides of mentorship. Over-reliance on a mentor can stifle your independence, and there's a risk of adopting outdated practices or biases. To fully benefit, you need to be in the right mindset for growth—self-aware enough to accept feedback and willing to put in the effort. A good mentor invests time in those committed to their development.

Tips for Finding a Mentor

When seeking a mentor, seek someone you trust who can offer objective guidance. While admiration for your mentor is beneficial, ensure they bring a diverse perspective. Seek wisdom derived from real-world experiences rather than theoretical knowledge. A great mentor helps you understand the *"why"* behind their lessons, making them relatable to your situation. Often, the best mentors enter your life without you even realizing it.

Mentorship is a powerful tool in leadership development. It involves defining clear goals, effective communication, absorbing wisdom, and putting in the effort. Mentorship transcends climbing the corporate ladder; it's about personal and professional growth. As we embark on this journey, let's be both learners and mentors, enriching the leadership community.

The Digital Age of Mentoring: Success in a Remote World

Working from home challenges us to communicate more thoughtfully. Instead of spontaneous office chats, we plan online meetings like virtual coffee, regular 1-on-1s, and video calls. This helps us stay connected while respecting everyone's need for focus time.

In this era of remote work, where the familiar sounds of offices have been replaced by the steady tapping of keyboards in kitchens, bedrooms, and home offices around the globe, the mentoring landscape is undergoing a similar shift. As mentors, we now find ourselves navigating virtual spaces, reshaping how we guide others, and fostering our professional connections. The essence of mentoring remains, involving guiding, inspiring, and challenging, urging mentors to use their keenly honed active listening skills to pick up on more verbal cues in this digital world, often confined to the 2-dimensional space of video calls.

Among the challenges, there are also opportunities. Remote work removes distance and barriers, making mentoring accessible to more people than ever. The bond between mentors and mentees now transcends geographical boundaries, evolving into a global experience.

As we navigate this digital age, mentoring isn't just adapting to new technology; it's reimagining how we connect with others. By embracing these changes, we adapt and thrive, ensuring that mentoring transcends physical boundaries to foster growth, confidence, and connection in this era of remote work. This serves as a call to action for mentors and mentees to embrace the change, believe in the power of mentorship, and surpass the limitations of yesterday.

The Mirrored Leadership Effect: Level up your Skills

In leadership, I've noticed a fascinating phenomenon—teams often mirror the behavior of their leader. This isn't just anecdotal; it's a reflection of how leadership style shapes a team's culture and performance.

If you think investing in your leadership skills doesn't matter, think again. Your leadership is mirrored back to you through your team's mindset, attitudes, and outcomes.

Types of Leaders and Their Reflections

The Toxic Leader

Toxic leaders operate from mistrust, believing their way is the only way. Data-driven analysis is used to prove their points, not to nurture growth. In this environment, teams mirror the leader's distrust. They second-guess themselves, fear mistakes, and work excessively—often at the cost of work-life balance and their overall well-being. High turnover and dissatisfaction become the norm, leading the team to burnout and dysfunction.

The Absent Leader

Absent leaders are focused on their own agenda, often overlooking their team's needs. They may hold weekly meetings, but these feel transactional: *"Here's what I need you to do this week."* Worse, these meetings are often canceled. The result? Disengaged teams mirror this neglect, doing just enough to get by but lacking motivation. Over time, the lack of leadership presence leads to a stagnant team with little forward momentum.

The Servant Leader

Servant leaders prioritize their people, investing in relationships and actively engaging with their team. They foster an atmosphere of trust and empowerment, where teams feel confident making decisions and learning from mistakes. Teams led by servant leaders mirror this investment, with a shared mantra of *"What if?"* driving creativity and pushing the team toward success and innovation.

The Emotionally Intelligent Leader

Leaders with high emotional intelligence (EI) see their team members as valued individuals, not just contributors. They create an environment where every voice matters, fostering a deep sense of psychological safety. Teams led with high EI mirror this inclusive culture, embracing diversity of thought and working cohesively, leading to high tenure, low turnover, and attracting new talent through referrals.

The Outlier

Of course, there are always outlier employees—those individuals who rebel, often because they haven't bought into the leader's vision. Addressing this buy-in early, giving your team transparent expectations and a clear vision can help, but more often than not, the mirror effect holds true.

A Reflection of You

I've seen the same team members behave drastically differently depending on who leads them. The same people, entirely different outcomes. If you want to understand your leadership style, start by observing your team. Reflect on their actions and attitudes as you are likely to see yourself in them. Focus on improving yourself, and you'll find your team naturally mirrors the example you set.

Changing Your Growth Potential

Have you ever wondered why change can feel scary? The truth is, our minds are wired for growth, yet we often view change as a threat. This tension—between staying the same and moving forward—offers an opportunity for reflection.

The Illusion of Staying the Same

People often resist change, but here's the paradox: staying the same is an illusion. Whether it's time, circumstances, or the quiet evolution of our thoughts, change is inevitable. What people resist isn't transformation—it's the discomfort that comes with it. When we create an environment where change feels natural, even empowering, it can feel almost comfortable.

Journey Back to Basics

What if life were simple? When you feel overwhelmed, returning to your roots may bring clarity. It can offer a fresh perspective, helping you see things more clearly—including the strengths and challenges that have shaped your story.

Here's a powerful reminder: you are not broken—you are enough. Strengths and weaknesses are part of your story, shaped by the challenges you've faced. Your experiences have made you stronger and reveal the potential within you. Limitations are simply obstacles waiting to be overcome.

Investing in Your Journey

You don't have to go it alone. Mentorship can accelerate growth by helping you recognize your strengths, guide you through challenges, and reveal your hidden potential.

A mentor helps you see the possibilities ahead, shares insights when you need them most, and supports you as you forge your own path. In this space of trust, you gain confidence and uncover your unique voice, empowering you to navigate challenges with clarity and purpose.

Alone, it's easy to feel stuck—like a hamster on a wheel, expending energy without direction. But with the right mentor, every step propels you forward, transforming potential into meaningful progress, allowing you to move forward with intention.

Habits: The Foundation of Mastery

Every change begins with repetition. The power of consistency is undeniable. Repetition creates habits, and habits shape who we aspire to be. Do it until it feels second nature. Whether it's a skill, a mindset, or a way of life, the path to mastery is paved with intention.

But habits are more than repetition—they need purpose to come to life. Humans are naturally curious, and when curiosity is sparked, focus follows. With focus comes the potential for meaningful change. Don't let the *"how"* hold you back—focus on igniting your *"why."* This gives you both direction and the motivation to get there.

What if you could reframe how you see change? When we align with our natural curiosity and create environments that support growth, resistance fades. Mentorship, habits, and personal reflection all converge—to inspire us to move forward with purpose. Change is inevitable, but the real question is whether we're ready to embrace the journey. *Are you?*

Mastering Outsourcing: Your Guide to a Successful Project

As a busy Tech Executive, I'm no stranger to the constant stream of pitches from outsourcing development companies looking to assist with my engineering needs. And let's face it—outsourcing can be a game-changer, whether it's a one-off project or a long-term partnership. But let's not sugarcoat it: while these firms might excel at writing code, many fall short when it comes to critical aspects of project management and the software development lifecycle.

The truth is, that expecting to hire an outsourcing company and then sit back while they handle everything is a recipe for disaster. Success in these projects isn't just about what you pay them—it's about the effort and involvement you put in.

You'd think that with the sheer volume of projects they handle, these service companies would have project management down to a science. But in my experience, that's rarely the case. They're often so focused on churning out projects that they overlook the finer details of effective project management.

So, where do they usually miss the mark? Let's break it down:

Project Management: From start to finish, projects require careful oversight. Milestone plans, deadlines, and meaningful status updates are essential. Risks must be addressed head-on, and they must be willing to bring in additional expertise if needed to keep projects on track.

Business Analysts: Having skilled business analysts onboard is essential, especially for projects with any user interaction. They're the ones who turn your requirements into actionable user stories, guiding the development process from stakeholder review to acceptance testing.

QA Test Cases: Unlike product companies, service-based firms often skip writing test cases. However, thorough testing is vital for ensuring the quality of the end product. Insist on proper test case documentation to ensure quality deliverables.

Thought Leadership: Don't settle for a transactional relationship. Post-project, outsourcing firms should offer fresh ideas and opportunities for further collaboration. After all, they're in a prime position to add ongoing value to your product.

Now that you have this knowledge, you're better prepared to work successfully with outsourcing firms, whether they're onshore, nearshore, or offshore. By applying these insights, you'll help ensure your projects are managed effectively and deliver the results you're aiming for. From my experience managing over $5 million in outsourced projects, I can say that staying involved is what turns a good investment into a great one.

Mastering Development Outsourcing: A Guide to Strategic Partnerships

If you are considering outsourcing your development work, approach the decision strategically. This means carefully weighing the benefits and potential drawbacks to see if it aligns with your overall business goals. When properly leveraged, outsourcing can significantly enhance efficiency and provide access to specialized expertise.

Decide to Outsource:

• One-time or Throwaway Projects: Development outsourcing is ideal for projects with a finite scope.

• Specialized Skillsets: Opt for outsourcing when the project demands specific skills that are not a long-term necessity for your team.

• Resource Constraints: Utilize outsourcing when your internal resources are insufficient to simultaneously handle ongoing efforts and project demands.

Select a Vendor:

• Long-Term Partnership: Seek a vendor who is committed to building lasting relationships, not just completing transactions.

• Deep Problem Insight: Choose a vendor who prioritizes understanding your specific challenges over blindly following preset solutions.

• Expertise Over Price: Opt for vendors based on their knowledge and ability to add value, rather than solely on cost.

• Honest Self-Assessment: Value partners who can honestly assess and communicate when a project is beyond their capabilities.

Project Engagement:

• Define Success Criteria: Clearly define success metrics upfront to align expectations and objectives.

• Comprehensive SoW or Contract: Formalize the partnership with a detailed Statement of Work or contract to clarify terms and responsibilities.

• Assume Project Leadership: Take an active leadership role to ensure the project aligns with your strategic goals.

• Skilled Project Management: Choose vendors with experienced project managers and business analysts who understand the importance of clear, actionable requirements.

• Collaborative Approach: Encourage a team mindset that integrates your staff and the vendor's team, avoiding an "us vs. them" dynamic.

• Milestone Definition: Establish clear milestones and deliverables to effectively monitor progress and ensure timely execution.

• Knowledge Transfer and Documentation: Require comprehensive knowledge transfer sessions and thorough documentation to maintain project continuity.

• Code Maintenance: Ensure that the developed code is maintainable and aligns with your team's capabilities for future modifications.

• IP Ownership: Secure intellectual property rights to protect your investments and innovations post-project.

By carefully considering these factors, you can establish a strong and strategic development outsourcing partnership that aligns with your business goals. From vendor selection to project leadership and knowledge transfer, each step plays a pivotal role in ensuring success. Leveraging my experience as a mentor and fractional tech executive, I have seen firsthand how these principles can guide teams toward effective outsourcing solutions.

Section 3

Communication & Influence

How leaders connect, guide, and inspire

Leading Through Questions: A Transformative Strategy

Getting your first leadership role means you've proven you're an outstanding team member. But did you know that effective leadership involves making yourself less essential? It might seem counterintuitive—why work so hard to get to a position only to make yourself unnecessary? This puzzling concept forever changed my approach to leadership.

When new members join my team, they're often surprised by how rarely I give direct answers. *"Why can't he just give me a straight answer so I can finish my work?"* they wonder. I once had a team leader remark, *"Jeffrey already knows the answers to most of the questions he asks."* So, why do I keep asking if I already know the answers? Because effective leadership is about transforming how people think, much like the old proverb suggests:

"Give a man a fish, and you feed him for a day. Teach a man to fish, and you feed him for a lifetime."

What Does It Mean to Lead Through Questions?

Leading through questions means empowering your team to solve problems on their own. You could be the person with all the answers, but then your team will always depend on you. What if you're not there? Teaching them to manage challenges without you prepares them for any situation they may encounter.

Your first step: drop the ego. Admit when you don't know something and encourage others to explore and express their thoughts. This approach builds a curious and learning-focused team, turning every challenge into an opportunity for growth.

Empowering Through Mindfulness

The next time you're asked for advice, flip the script: *"What do you think?"* or *"What would you do if this were your company?"* Encouraging these questions helps team members develop independent thinking and strengthens their confidence in decision-making. This mindfulness nurtures their ability to reflect on and manage their thoughts and promotes a culture where making thoughtful, autonomous decisions is valued.

Stay patient, especially if there is resistance—employ emotional intelligence to gauge the situation and respond appropriately. Try presenting a few options and discuss which one seems best. If their choice aligns with yours, accept their decision and explain why it makes sense. If not, explore the benefits and drawbacks of each option, providing new insights and perspectives.

Occasionally, your team will propose ideas that differ from yours. Allowing them to test their strategies fosters innovation and refines their problem-solving skills.

A Message to Aspiring Leaders

If you're new to leadership and these concepts seem confusing, don't worry. Reaching a point where your team no longer relies on your constant input is a sign of leadership success. This independence opens doors for you to explore further opportunities for your own career growth.

A Simple Question of Effective Leadership

Have you ever felt like you were asked a question that simply left you with more questions? Leadership is as much about the questions we ask as the decisions we make. A recent mentoring session with Jamie—a leader in their field—demonstrated how a simple question can either undermine or enhance team confidence.

In a status meeting, a senior leader asked, *"How confident are you that your team will meet the deadline?"* This seemingly simple question implied doubt, causing Jamie to worry unnecessarily for two days about what they might have overlooked.

To address this concern, I reframed the question during our mentoring session: *"In percentages, how confident are you that you will meet the deadline?"* Jamie's response, *"80%,"* and clarified that their confidence hinged on another team's timely cooperation. This shift in perspective helped them move from anxiety to a clear action plan.

Jamie's project involved:
- Five tasks fully within the team's control
- Three tasks slightly dependent on another team
- Two tasks heavily reliant on cooperation with another team

The strategy was straightforward: view the other team as partners essential for collaborative success, not as separate entities. This approach minimizes stress by prioritizing tasks based on dependency levels and proactively managing interactions. After a quick conversation, the leader of the other team understood that their shared goal depended on cooperation and was more than willing to assist.

Effective leadership is fundamentally about communication—asking questions that build confidence rather than sow doubt. By intentionally altering how you ask questions, you can develop a culture of collaboration, remove obstacles, and guide your team toward success. As a leader, consider this: Are your questions sowing doubt or are they cultivating confidence and cooperation?

The Deadline Trap: A Simple Question Transforms Leadership

The Trap

Imagine this scenario: as a leader, I ask you, *"When can you have that report to me?"* Without hesitation, you quickly assess your team's workload, juggle priorities, and confidently respond, *"I can have it to you within the next two hours."* You rush back to your team, inform them that the boss needs this report immediately, and disrupt their focus to deliver it on time.

But did this really add value? Consider the potential cost in productivity and team morale. The truth is, that many leaders fall into the trap of assuming urgency without first clarifying the actual deadline. A far more effective approach would be to simply ask, *"When do you need it?"*

Clear Expectations

This question opens the door to clearer expectations. If the response is, *"I need it in an hour,"* it fundamentally changes the conversation. You might quickly realize that delivering a comprehensive report within that time frame isn't feasible. This provides an opportunity to set clear expectations or propose an alternative that better aligns with your team's capacity, without compromising quality.

Ask the Right Questions

Now, think about the opposite scenario. What if I said, *"I need it by the end of the month?"* You might feel confident that you can deliver the report well before then—let's say, by the end of next week. You confidently accomplish the goal and meet the deadline. However, upon delivery, you discover that the data is incomplete because it doesn't cover the final weeks of the month. Once again, assumptions led to misalignment.

Take a Balanced Approach

Balancing the quality of the deliverable with the time available is key. Maybe it takes two days to build a presentation with all the bells and whistles—graphs, images, impactful statistics, and even video testimonials. But is all of that truly necessary? By asking for both the deadline and a clear picture of what success looks like, you ensure your team's efforts are directed at delivering the most meaningful results without wasted time or effort.

Benefit from Flow and Efficiency

Ready to transform the way you lead? Start by asking, *"When do you need it?"* in your next conversation and observe the difference it makes. It's more than just managing deadlines—it builds a culture of open communication and sets the stage for realistic expectations. By aligning your team's efforts with clear deadlines, you minimize disruptions and create an environment where focus, flow, and efficiency are valued. Your team and leadership will both thank you.

Understanding Feedback: Planting the Seeds of Positive Growth

Feedback and criticism are terms often used interchangeably, yet they differ fundamentally in intent and impact. Understanding these distinctions can transform our interactions and build a mindset for growth and optimism.

Criticism versus Feedback: A Simple Example

Consider two similar scenarios between a couple of boys:
Criticism: Boy 1 tells Boy 2, *"You are so stupid, you're doing that wrong!"* Here, Boy 1 aims to elevate himself by belittling Boy 2, driven by selfish motives.
Feedback: Observing Boy 2's struggle, Boy 1 offers, *"Let me show you a better way to do this."* This approach is selfless—Boy 1's goal is to aid Boy 2, providing improvement without any direct personal gain.

This contrast highlights that while considering the motive behind feedback—the *"why"*—is more critical than the *"what."*

The Essence of Constructive Feedback

Constructive feedback isn't about boosting the giver's self-esteem; it's about genuinely aiding the recipient's development. True feedback is a gift of growth, delivered with goodwill and mutual respect, intended to promote improvement and foster excellence. Shifting our focus from self-serving criticism to selfless feedback helps create a culture that values growth, respect, and collaboration.

The Role of Positivity in Growth

Growth requires a delicate balance between challenge and support. Negativity often stifles potential, while positivity serves as a catalyst for improvement.

Consider this challenge I use in my mentoring sessions:
"Prove to me that you didn't drink coffee today."

This exercise highlights the futility of focusing only on negatives. Growth comes about by actively reinforcing and acting on positives. But *"Why?"*

Providing effective feedback involves explaining its benefits. By helping the recipient understand the value feedback brings, you enable them to frame it positively in their mind. Offering the *"why"* along with the *"what"* lowers defenses and fosters receptivity to feedback while at the same time giving them a goal to achieve.

Planting Seeds of Growth

In mentoring, my mentees often like to give me credit, but in reality, they are the ones who do all the work. Giving feedback can be likened to planting seeds, then stepping back and watching them grow. Just as a sapling needs soil, water, and sunlight to grow, giving feedback is like giving encouragement, guidance, and the right conditions to grow. But ultimately, they must harness these resources themselves to develop and thrive.

By recognizing the true nature and power of feedback, we can reframe our approach to interactions, boosting both individual growth and our collective success. Next time you give feedback, reflect on your motivations to determine whether you are merely criticizing or providing genuine feedback.

Critical Leadership: Designing Feedback for Growth

Have you recently reviewed your team's work and praised them with *"great job!"*? While this approach avoids nitpicking small nuances and might seem supportive, ask yourself: Is this truly serving your team's growth, or could it be doing more harm than good?

The Pitfalls of *"Great Job!"*

As leaders, our responsibility is to challenge our team, continually pushing them to become the best versions of themselves. Gentle praise, while positive, can limit their growth by not encouraging them to stretch themselves and improve their skills.

Learn from Engineering

Consider the *"Critical Design Review"* used in engineering, where the focus is on potential failures rather than successes. This process demands critical thinking and often brings in fresh perspectives to spot overlooked flaws. Such rigorous scrutiny, required in high-stakes environments, can be a powerful tool in leadership feedback.

Adopting a New Approach

By adopting this engineering-inspired approach to feedback, we can significantly enhance our team's resilience and growth. It involves strategically timing praise to maximize its impact and promote continuous improvement.

The Power of Constructive Feedback

Balance your feedback using your emotional intelligence. It should be constructive, targeting the work and not the person, your goal is to educate and guide rather than to criticize or blame. Consistently focusing on areas for improvement helps uphold higher standards and builds a culture and environment where excellence becomes the norm.

The Iterative Process of Review

Reviews should be iterative, aimed at continuous improvement rather than arbitrary changes. Provide understanding through your critiques, helping your team with clear expectations and direction. Once they grasp the *"why"* behind the feedback, they will be better equipped to achieve success. The goal is to define clear objectives and assist the team in reaching them, ensuring they are never left guessing.

Strategically Offer Praise

When your team surpasses expectations, that's the ideal time to offer unexpected praise in a manner that motivates and rewards excellence. This acknowledgment can reinforce their success and boost their morale, leaving them feeling valued for their hard work.

Reflect and Challenge

Consider this: *Are you merely allowing your team to settle for "good enough," or are you actively pushing them toward new heights with insightful, constructive feedback?*

Aim to perfect the art of feedback to build resilience and excellence within your team. It's about finding the right balance—knowing precisely how to challenge and when to praise. Embrace this model, and watch your team's potential unfold.

Mastering the Art of Effortless Communication

Have you ever been captivated by someone who explains complex ideas with ease? Their words flow smoothly, leaving you with crystal-clear understanding. This isn't magic—it's the art of cognitive communication.

Think of cognitive communication as listening to a beautiful piece of music being played on a piano. The goal is to align your message with how the human mind processes information. It creates an enchanting stream of musical notes that your audience can effortlessly follow. Let's explore how you too can master this technique.

Creating a Cognitive Goal

Offer a clear goal, like providing your audience a program to follow. Knowing the destination makes the journey easier. This can be a clear title telling them what they are about to learn.

Engaging Curiosity

Begin with an intriguing question or statement. Like a powerful beginning to a musical piece, it can engage people at an emotional level. This engages curiosity and opens their minds to new ideas—they want to hear more.

Breaking Down Complexity

Transform complex ideas into smaller, digestible parts. Think of learning the piano: you begin with a few simple keys and chords, then master more as you go along. Help your audience by teaching them your complex concept in a way that they can master each key piece at a time.

The Secret of Analogies

Analogies are your secret weapon to connect new ideas to familiar ones—like hearing your favorite song on the radio. Isn't it easier to recall lyrics than it was to learn them the first time? Just remember, the more relatable the analogy, the easier the connection for your audience.

Conversational Tone and Natural Pauses

Maintain a conversational tone as if you're chatting with a friend; this builds trust and keeps your audience engaged. Incorporate natural pauses for reflection—these moments allow for the absorption of knowledge. Don't be afraid of silence, you don't have to fill every moment with words. In a musical piece, silence can be as powerful as the notes.

The Power of Positivity

Keep your words positive. Present challenges as opportunities for growth; this keeps your audience open and receptive to new ideas. Even though you are presenting them with new information, it also becomes an art of subtle persuasion.

Storytelling

As a communicator, you're responsible for your audience's journey. Like a skilled musician, take them on a journey with a beginning, middle, and end. Comprehension is a gateway to understanding. Watch for indications of confusion and adjust your pace accordingly.

Employing these techniques will help your ideas flow more smoothly into others' minds. You'll build understanding to a crescendo, making complexity feel simple.

Next time you speak, ask yourself: How can I make this experience seamless and rewarding for my audience?

That's the essence of mastering cognitive communication—and you already have the instruments—your mind and your voice.

A First-Class Ticket to Getting People On Board

Do you ever feel frustrated trying to convince others of your ideas? You're not alone. Persuasion can be a complex skill to master, but with the right strategies, you can guide others to see the value in your proposals.

Know Your Audience

To effectively persuade others, the first step is to know your audience. This means putting yourself in their shoes and considering their perspectives and pressures. By understanding their point of view, you can tailor your approach in a way that shows real value for them. Establishing the relevance of your proposal early on is key; quickly explaining why your idea matters will capture their attention and encourage them to listen.

Build Trust

Building trust and rapport is another essential component of persuasion. Demonstrating honesty and transparency builds a sense of trust, making people more receptive to your message. It's also important to listen to their doubts and uncertainties. By showing that you value their opinions and acknowledge their points, you create a better rapport that enhances overall communication.

The Power of Clarity

When it comes to communicating your idea, clarity can be empowering. Use straightforward language to ensure your message is easily understood while avoiding jargon or overly complex explanations that might confuse your audience. Presenting both the pros and cons of your idea allows you to explain your proposal effectively, demonstrating that you've thought it through while addressing potential objections with confidence.

Confidence is King

Exuding confidence in your proposal can significantly influence others' perceptions. If you believe in your idea, this belief becomes contagious; conversely, hesitation can lead to doubt among your audience. Supporting your arguments with factual data rather than personal opinions further strengthens your position—facts are hard to dispute.

An Action Plan

Finally, encourage action and next steps. Providing a clear plan for implementing your idea reduces ambiguity and helps others feel more comfortable committing to change. Additionally, creating a sense of choice can be effective; when people feel they have options, it often reduces resistance. Providing choice allows them to feel a sense of control and can lead to a greater willingness to get on board with your proposal.

Think of yourself as the captain of a boat. Getting people on board means looking at it from their perspective. They don't need to know everything you know—just enough to alleviate their fears and doubts. Once you help them recognize that you are trustworthy and have a clear plan, they will be more inclined to join you on this journey.

By weaving these strategies into your approach, you can enhance your persuasive abilities and significantly increase the likelihood of gaining support for your ideas. Give some thought about how you get people on board with your ideas.

A Question of Thought Leadership

A curious student asked a seemingly simple question: *"How do you become a thought leader?"* At first glance, it seems straightforward, but the answer reveals a profound journey—one defined by insight, influence, and intellectual growth.

With so much information at our fingertips, the real challenge is sifting through it all to uncover meaningful insights. Thought leaders don't simply follow the flow of ideas—they redirect it. They challenge assumptions, inspire progress, and illuminate new possibilities. Yet, the path to thought leadership isn't about reaching a destination—it's about embracing a lifelong pursuit of discovery.

Igniting the Spark

Thought leadership begins with a spark—a moment when curiosity and expertise converge to illuminate a fresh perspective. A thought leader sees connections where others see only fragments, transforming ideas into insights that reframe the world. This spark grows into a vision that inspires others to question assumptions and explore new possibilities.

But a spark alone isn't enough. Credibility must follow, forged through deep exploration, rigorous study, and the courage to ask hard questions.

Leadership thrives on trust, built on integrity—owning your knowledge, acknowledging your limits, and committing to continuous growth. These qualities transform insights into ideas others are eager to embrace.

Impact Through Influence

True influence isn't about pushing one's ideas on others; it's about clarity. Thought leaders act like a magnifying glass, refining their message to bring focus and sparking communities to amplify their voice. Their message ignites collective thought, spreading into a legacy of shared understanding and action.

The Power of Storytelling

A thought leader's ability to connect with others is as important as their ideas. Like a well-written book, storytelling takes the audience on a journey—navigating challenges, uncovering insights, and building toward moments of clarity. Along the way, thought leaders simplify complexity, guiding their audience to understanding and action. In the end, they reveal what matters most: an idea made simple, resonant, and transformative.

The Endless Journey

The answer for the curious student is simple—thought leadership is not a title, but a mindset. It's about embracing curiosity, challenging assumptions, and continually exploring uncharted ideas.

It takes confidence and clarity to step into the public eye, paired with an openness to engage with contrasting perspectives. Thought leadership is a mindset—a willingness to be wrong and to view those moments as opportunities for growth. A true thought leader is an information collector, always seeking new knowledge and refining their understanding, leading to clarity and insight along our journey of life.

Beyond Comparison: Setting the Standard for Innovation

Back when I first launched my own product, my team proudly showed me a slide where we outshone all our competitors. According to that slide, we were the best of the best, better than all the rest. I made a decision: I told my team to scrap that slide, and never to show it to me again. *Why?* Because I didn't want us to be the *"me too"* and have all the same features as everyone else. I didn't want us to focus on being better than others; I wanted us to be the best version of ourselves.

See, it's easy to get caught up in the competition, constantly comparing ourselves to others. But that's not how you truly innovate. My vision was clear: ignore the noise, tackle industry challenges head-on, and become the benchmark others aspire to.

I envisioned a future where competitors would scramble to catch up, crafting comparison slides to measure up to our product.

The key takeaway? *Don't settle for being an imitation. Be the trailblazer, the one setting the bar for excellence.*

Confident Leadership: A Point of View

In a coaching session, a new CEO was reflecting on a recent meeting with his team. He was pleased—he had given them what he thought was good advice, sharing how he would approach their task. He saw it as helpful insight. I saw a problem.

The Unhelpful Advice

Great leaders understand perspective—they excel at putting themselves in someone else's shoes. So, I asked him, *"If your team finds a better way to do this, what do they do?"*

"They do it their way," he replied.

"Are you sure?" I pushed. *"Or do they stop and ask themselves: Do I do it my way or the CEO's way? He's the leader, it's his company... but don't I know my job better than he does."*

See the conflict you just created? That hesitation? That's the damage. A team member who now second-guesses their own expertise because the CEO—who holds power over their future—offered helpful advice.

You hired them to do their job. Do you trust them to do it? If so, then trust starts with quiet confidence.

Understand Your Role, and Theirs

Being a CEO is hard! As a leader, your job is to support your team—ensuring they have what they need to succeed. You set the vision, mission, north star, and expectations for outcomes—but when you weigh in on how the work gets done, even with the best intentions, something subtle happens. That moment of guidance can quietly undermine everything you've been building.

Trust erodes—both the trust you have in them and the trust they have in themselves.

I know, this may sound counterintuitive. Maybe you could do their job better than them. Perhaps you do have more experience. But how will they improve if they don't trust themselves enough to learn?

The Ripple Effect

Now, fast-forward. What happens the next time that employee gets stuck?

Do they trust that you believe in them? Do they take ownership and figure it out? Or do they hesitate—waiting, second-guessing, wondering if they should check in with you first?

See the problem?

The moment we tell them how to do their job, we introduce doubt. We erode their confidence. They hesitate when they should act.

Set Expectations—Then Step Back

Give your team clear expectations. Empower them to be successful. Give them a clear vision—a North Star—to make confident decisions on their own. Stop at the moment you want to tell them how to do their job.

Some unsolicited advice? Ask better questions:
• Do you understand the outcome we are looking for?
• Do you have what you need to be successful?

These questions reinforce trust. They remind your team that you hired them for a reason—and that you believe in their ability to deliver.

The advice I gave this CEO was to remember, in that moment: The most powerful thing a leader can say is nothing at all.

Section 4

Culture & Environment

Creating the space where teams thrive

Navigating Successfully Through Inclusive Leadership

Embrace Equality and True Diversity:

As you step into your leadership journey, learn to truly value the distinctive strengths of each team member. Discard the idea of labels; what counts is supporting each individual's success. In an inclusive workplace, champion diverse thoughts, ensure everyone has a voice, and encourage constructive debate. Recognize and genuinely value each team member's contributions. Cultivate an environment where your team feels both encouraged and empowered to share thoughts and ideas, fostering a space for collaboration and continual growth.

Focus on Transparency and Growth:

As you navigate the path to success, prioritize open communication. Offer constructive feedback to individuals on your team, recognizing their strengths and areas for improvement while keeping them informed about their progress. This transparency eliminates confusion, establishing clear expectations and fostering an environment where individuals feel valued and secure. Authentic leadership, staying true to yourself, cultivates a shared understanding, and your team will reflect your genuine approach. Foster a culture of open dialogue, where feedback becomes a valuable tool for continual improvement and growth.

Trust and Verify:

Enhance your team's capabilities by fostering trust while emphasizing the importance of verification. When your team feels valued and supported, their resilience and productivity naturally rise. Trust forms a sturdy foundation, instilling confidence in individuals to confront challenges, spark innovation, and glean valuable lessons from failures, leading to overall success. Seamlessly incorporate measurement and validation into your approach – improvement is more achievable when measured. Make trust a priority and assess outcomes; this dual focus will pave the way for your team's success.

Leading Remote Teams:

Although leading a remote workforce might seem daunting, effective leadership goes beyond physical location. Success with global teams hinges on clear communication, trust, and a genuine appreciation for each team member. It's not about where they are but rather how you lead. Break down geographical barriers by emphasizing inclusivity, transparency, trust, and productivity. As you lead with these principles, your journey to success transforms into an exciting shared adventure, regardless of the miles that may separate you.

Success Through Inclusive Leadership: Diversity and Collaboration

There are countless books on leadership, yet one thing remains clear: the role of a leader has changed dramatically. Recently, while applying for a CTO role, the CEO summed up expectations for me in one word: *"Inspire."* Today's leaders must do more than manage—they must inspire their teams, promote diversity, and encourage collaboration. Here, I'll share some practical tips on how these skills are essential for building a culture of innovation.

Equality and True Diversity

Effective leadership appreciates each individual's uniqueness. Going beyond just avoiding stereotypes, involves actively nurturing a culture where everyone's unique capabilities are recognized and valued. True diversity moves past mere labels to embrace the wide variety of perspectives and skills each team member brings. Encouraging diverse thoughts and inclusivity helps leaders cultivate a collaborative culture where every individual has the chance to thrive.

Transparency as a Cornerstone

Transparency is essential for effective leadership. Leaders benefit from their own self-awareness and authenticity. Leading by example encourages teams to mirror this behavior, fostering an environment where everyone feels acknowledged and encouraged to share their ideas and concerns. Although transparency may occasionally cause discomfort, it can lead to clearer communication and stronger mutual understanding. By being transparent and clear with expectations, leaders can nurture trust within their organization.

Build Trust for Psychological Safety

To unlock your team's full potential, start by demonstrating trust in your team members. This approach builds their confidence in your leadership—people follow leaders they believe in. Guide your team to experience the benefits of mutual trust: it enhances collaboration and boosts productivity. When teams operate in an environment of trust that supports psychological safety, it naturally leads to higher performance.

Leading Remote Teams

Physical distance doesn't have to hinder productivity. Effective remote leadership makes geographic boundaries irrelevant by prioritizing clear communication, trust, and appreciation for each team member's contributions. The success of a team depends more on having an effective leader than on any location. Use specific tools and strategies to keep communication clear and ensure every team member feels connected and valued, regardless of where they are.

These strategies demonstrate how leaders can thrive by adapting and upholding values of authenticity and trust. Leadership is about continuous growth; focus on these principles to bring inclusivity and diversity to your organization. Consider how you can integrate transparency into your leadership style. Embrace these skills to foster a culture that inspires productivity, encourages collaboration, and celebrates diversity.

The Neurodivergent Paradox: Embracing Challenges to Uncover Hidden Strengths

I have the privilege of mentoring gifted children, and it's a journey where I often question who gains more from our interactions – them or me. Working with gifted individuals is both eye-opening and immensely fulfilling, although it can be a challenge to understand their neurodivergent minds. Being neurodivergent presents its own set of challenges and benefits. Let's consider the following:

Challenge: Mental Escapades

Some of them create intricate worlds in their minds, which can lead to daydreaming and a perceived lack of focus. They may see the world like looking through a kaleidoscope.

Benefit: Cognitive Flexibility

Yet, this ability to visualize concepts in 360 degrees may lead to innovative problem-solving skills, offering fresh perspectives that often lead to groundbreaking solutions.

Challenge: Sensory Overload

They may struggle with sensory overload in crowded environments, leading to feelings of isolation and anxiety.

Benefit: Hyper-Focus

However, this can lead to hyper-focus and allow them to hone in on tasks with incredible precision, developing neural pathways that excel in compartmentalization and rapid context switching.

Challenge: Communication Hurdles

Their rapid thought processes may outpace their ability to say what's on their minds or manifest in conditions like dysgraphia.

Benefit: Exceptional Memory

This can lead to heightened cognitive activity and allow exceptional memory retention and recall, with individuals adopting their own form of shorthand to keep pace with their thoughts.

Challenge: Racing Thoughts

Their minds may be filled with ideas and seem like seeing the world through the lens of an infinity mirror. This can lead to an appearance of slower processing when in reality their minds are running at a faster pace and processing so much more information.

Benefit: Rapid Analysis

Yet, they can learn to analyze situations and concepts with amazing speed. They can possess the ability to make mental connections with divergent ideas by bringing together seemingly unrelated concepts in a way that only a mind like this can see.

Challenge: Social Adaptation

They may find it challenging to connect with neurotypical peers, especially in group settings, due to difficulties in mutual understanding.

Benefit: Genuine Connections

When they do form bonds, these relationships are often profound and enduring. Some even possess a remarkable ability to adapt and empathize, effortlessly blending in like a chameleon to relate to others.

Encountering a neurodivergent individual is like discovering a rare gem; they have the power to expand your perspectives and challenge your assumptions in ways you never thought possible. The good news is that you don't have to understand how their minds work to call them your friend. Become an advocate for the neurodivergent and let them excel.

The Strength in Imperfection: Rethinking Leadership and Team Dynamics

Some may describe *"leadership"* as decisive action and impeccable strategy. Many good leaders are often perfectionists, constantly striving for more, for better, for perfection! However, becoming a truly effective leader might require becoming comfortable with imperfection.

Here is a quote of my own: *"Sometimes, perfection is imperfect, and imperfect is perfection."*

This mindset is particularly relevant in leadership, showing us that the best teams might evolve from the least polished beginnings.

Valuing Imperfect Decisions

As a leader, it can be tempting to view your ideas as the only correct ones and steer your team's ideas toward your own. Yet, this can restrict the creative potential and independent thought processes of your diverse team. Unlock unexpected successes and foster innovative solutions by allowing imperfect decisions—opportunities that a more controlled approach might never reveal.

Fostering a Growth Mindset

True leadership is not measured by flawless execution but by the ability to inspire and empower others to develop their independent ideas. By stepping back and allowing team members to explore their own initiatives—even when they differ from yours—you nurture a growth mindset where innovation and collaboration are the priority.

The Paradox of Perfection in Leadership

The concept of perfection in leadership is simple. By accepting and even encouraging less polished ideas, a team can become more adaptable, creative, and resilient. Viewing imperfection as an asset often serves as an ideal model, leading to more collaborative team dynamics and a highly effective organizational culture.

Building a Foundation for Success

The perfectionism that propelled you into leadership must now evolve to prioritize your team's collective success. As a leader, your effectiveness hinges on their achievements. By allowing your team the freedom to propose and experiment with imperfect ideas, you set the stage for developing the perfect team over time.

Embracing Failure: A Path to Innovation and Success

In this journey of life, where we often encounter the advice that *"failure is not an option,"* both as a mentor and engineer, I've come to realize that this notion is not only unrealistic but counterproductive. As you walk through life, in any field, keep in mind this simple key to true innovation and success: it lies in embracing failure as a necessary stepping stone toward greatness.

Drawing inspiration from the wisdom of Thomas Edison, one of history's greatest inventors, we find that his mastery in embracing failure paved the way for numerous groundbreaking inventions. Each failure brought valuable lessons, contributing more to his success than any of his triumphs. In the world of engineering, failure is not a setback; instead, engineers expect and embrace it as an integral part of the process.

Take this moment, to reflect on your own experiences. How many attempts did it take to master seemingly simple tasks like tying your shoes or riding a bike? As a leader, how many times did you stumble before finding your way? The path to success is often paved with failures, and every misstep is a badge of honor.

So, would you rather be the one who invented the light bulb on the first try or the one who, like Edison, tried 100 times before achieving success? Embracing failure is not a sign of weakness but a testament to your determination and willingness to learn. Ultimately, it's through failures that we evolve into the innovators and leaders we aspire to be. Let's rewrite the well-intentioned advice to *"Failure is necessary"* and consider it a mantra to carry along your path to success.

What It Means to Live Without Ego

One of my mentees once asked me, *"How do I live without ego? Does it mean never talking about myself? Never taking credit for my achievements?"*

I smiled—it's a deceptively simple question—one that many wrestle with, especially in leadership. For years, I've lived by the principle of eliminating my ego because I've come to see it adds no real value. But what does that actually mean?

It's About Intention

Living without ego isn't about fading into the background or diminishing yourself—it's about the why behind your actions. Ego emerges when your intent shifts toward boasting, misleading, or manipulating others for personal gain—selfish intentions.

Let's take an everyday example. If you're trying to bring someone on board with your idea, living without ego means presenting the facts that lead them to the same conclusion—not bending reality to serve your narrative. In the process, you may even gain a new perspective yourself. When your intention is to help others make an informed decision rather than to manipulate, ego takes a backseat.

Internal Validation

Here's the thing, living without ego doesn't mean denying yourself credit. It means owning who you are and what you contribute—living authentically.

If you deserve a raise, help your leadership team recognize that truth. Present the facts: the results you've driven, the challenges you've overcome, and the value you've added. Let data guide the conversation. When recognition is rooted in honesty and collaboration, it becomes a win-win.

Living without an ego means your accomplishments stand on their own. They're grounded in facts, undeniable, and independent of external validation.

A Leader's Perspective

As a leader, I measure my success through the achievements of my team. When they succeed, it reflects the role I've played in removing obstacles, supporting their growth, and creating opportunities. Our accomplishments are a shared triumph because we all played our part.

Ego-free leadership celebrates shared progress and collective success. It's about focusing on the team's accomplishments rather than seeking personal validation. I feel pride in my team for the success we've achieved, knowing we've all contributed to the journey.

True Alignment

Living without ego means living with intention. It's about aligning your actions with authenticity, with motivations rooted in truth and purpose.

Be honest. Be intentional. Be open. The ego thrives on exaggeration, but a life anchored in sincerity is grounded in reality—your simple truth is enough.

So, how do you live without ego? Confidently own your contributions. Let your values be reflected in your actions. Show up as your best self, guided by truth, openness, and purpose.

Why Winning Teams Still Lose

"Our team is doing great!"

These are confident words. Yet, I see a problem. They see themselves as a separate team.

Silos wear down the company's productivity by creating false confidence.

The product is delayed—again. Marketing is waiting on Delivery. Delivery is waiting on Quality Control. Who is chasing the requirements that changed three weeks ago? And nobody saw it coming, because everyone was doing their part.

High-functioning teams can still fail if they only succeed independently.

Every team has clear goals. Meetings stay focused. People stay in their lane. From the inside, it feels efficient.

But, is it?

They should be saying, *"Our company is doing great!"* An organization only wins when everyone works together.

What Silos Miss

Teams are often measured by output. Tasks get completed, and requirements are met. Reports show progress, and KPIs are in the green. Teams are traditionally taught to focus on what they can control.

From their perspective, everything looks on track. The processes are documented. Timelines are being met. Daily tasks become routine—everyone knows what to do.

But once the deliverables move downstream, a different picture emerges. Priorities don't align. Requirements have shifted. Dependencies surfaced that were never discussed.

Big picture—each team is doing well, while the organization struggles. These breakdowns stem from the way the work is measured. Each team is optimizing in isolation, without full awareness of who's affected or what else is in motion.

The System Begins to Fracture

Unfortunately, breakdowns are rarely noticed until it's too late.

They begin early—when a dependency gets missed, a quick call to keep things moving, a shortcut to hit a deadline. These moments seem minor—a small change no one expected to matter. And the work continues, unaware that something's already gone off track.

But, did anyone ask if the decision was made with full visibility?

Without big-picture awareness, these shifts go unnoticed. Progress continues from team to team, but the connection across them weakens over time.

Trust begins to erode. Each team feels they've done their part—so when things go wrong, silos are created and deepened.

Each team was successful—yet, the outcome was still flawed.

Working With Alignment

Removing silos strengthens the system—building trust while improving outcomes.

Teams that operate with shared visibility adjust earlier. They align with those defining the requirements. They coordinate timing with the teams that follow. And they make confident decisions—grounded in awareness of who depends on what, and when.

This clarity improves delivery. Handoffs carry context. Rework is avoided. Progress continues without disruption.

The result leads to a scalable system. Teams deliver with confidence—organizational trust grows as people experience collaboration and support. Alignment becomes the new measure of success.

Enabling the True Potential of HR and IT

Throughout my career, I've observed how external pressures can sometimes push HR and IT teams into defensive, gatekeeping roles. When *"No"* becomes the default response, valuable opportunities for growth and innovation are often lost. It's important to recognize that these key departments hold tremendous potential to drive an organization's success. The most effective HR and IT teams I've encountered operate under a guiding principle: they're there to help.

IT: Beyond Infrastructure to Empowerment

An IT organization provides mission-critical support, ensuring each employee has the tools to perform at their best. From maintaining technology infrastructure and securing systems against cyber threats to managing data access, IT teams safeguard an organization's digital ecosystem. However, the most impactful IT teams go beyond their technical focus—when it comes to assisting employees, they start with *"Yes."*

Successful IT teams embrace their position as enablers, cutting through technological complexity to create a streamlined experience for those they support. Their goal is to simplify work, reducing the frustration often associated with complex systems. By effectively guiding staff in utilizing technology, IT drives both efficiency and productivity.

HR: A Human-Centric Approach

HR organizations hold a deeply specialized responsibility, requiring nuanced knowledge of employment laws, benefits, and the entire employee lifecycle. When HR teams focus solely on protecting the company, they limit their potential for positive impact.

Truly effective HR teams place *"Humans"* at the center of their *"Human Resources"* mindset. In today's tech-driven world, people remain a company's most valuable asset. Creating a psychologically safe environment allows employees to feel respected and heard. By building trust and prioritizing human capital management, HR lays the groundwork for a loyal, engaged workforce—one where employees feel valued and motivated to build long-term careers within the organization.

The Mindset of Service

Both HR and IT play vital roles in empowering employees. When these teams view employees as internal customers and adopt a service mindset, they bring empathy and professionalism to the workforce. Encourage your teams to prioritize clear communication and approach each request with *"How can I help?"* This collaborative mindset can transform how employees experience and engage with their work.

The reward for this approach? A culture of mutual respect, gratitude, and high performance. HR and IT professionals who see their mission as serving others contribute significantly to organizational success.

People Behind the Metrics

Have you ever wondered what truly drives employee engagement, and ultimately employee retention? Is it the metrics and KPIs we so often use to gauge the health of our organizations, or is it something deeper—something immeasurable yet undeniably more powerful?

The Numbers

I am a firm believer in: *"what is measured can be improved."* While metrics are invaluable for tracking progress, they only tell part of the story. Beneath the surface lies a deeper reality: employees are humans. To them, trust, purpose, and fulfillment matter more than your numbers.

We tend to measure what's easiest to track: hours worked, tasks completed, and revenue generated. Imagine a scoreboard—it shows who's winning, but does it reveal how the players feel about the game? These metrics paint a picture but often miss the human values that breathe life into an organization and shape its culture. What about collaboration, innovation, or a sense of belonging? These immeasurable factors often determine whether employees stay engaged or quietly check out.

What Matters

Consider two employees in similar roles. Both meet their KPIs, delivering on expectations. But one thrives—eager to collaborate, excited by their work, deeply invested in the team's success—while the other disengages, feeling unrecognized and disconnected. Traditional metrics might flag them both as high performers, but only one truly embodies engagement. Why does this happen? How can we address this?

Engagement Through Conversations

Retaining career employees dedicated to your company's success starts with understanding what fulfills them. Sitting down with employees allows you to uncover these qualitative factors. Things like flexible schedules, wellness programs, and a healthy work-life balance play a key role. These quality-of-life factors are often overlooked but can determine whether employees thrive, quietly disengage, or simply leave.

Sit down with each employee, engage in open, meaningful conversations, and hear their stories. Use this time to uncover what drives their engagement and identify opportunities for meaningful change. They may reveal how leadership styles, team dynamics, and workplace culture impact morale while building trust and collaboration. Act on what you learn to create a workplace where employees feel valued and motivated to thrive.

Balancing the Quantitative and Qualitative

Good leaders balance the qualitative with the quantitative. Survey scores point to trends, but open-ended comments and conversations uncover the *"why,"* leading to actionable outcomes. By understanding and addressing what truly matters, you will inspire your team.

Moving beyond metrics means focusing on what truly drives success: *people*. Create an environment where employees feel seen, valued, and empowered. Think about the team you want—individuals meeting metrics while quietly planning their next move, or dedicated employees deeply invested in your company's success.

Section 5

Decision-Making & Execution

Leading toward effective outcomes

Effective Strategies for Group Decision-Making

Navigating group decisions can be overwhelming, like weaving through a bustling marketplace of ideas. But with the right strategies, it's manageable. How can we guide a group to a decisive decision while ensuring everyone's voice is heard? Here are some practical strategies I often teach to new leaders under my mentorship:

Elect a Leader: Before diving into discussions, designate a trusted leader, for the group to make the final call. Ideally, this leader is the team's subject matter expert on the topic at hand. Their expertise can guide the conversation while ensuring decisions are informed and strategically sound.

Majority Rules: Another effective approach is the principle of majority rule. However, be cautious of potential drawbacks, such as marginalizing minority opinions. Ensure an odd number of participants to avoid ties, allowing the majority to dictate the course of action. In the case of an even number of group members, consider electing someone to be a moderator to guide the conversation and ensure open communication for all voices to be heard and considered.

North Star: Use a North Star approach by beginning with a clear goal for the decision. Write down the goal(s) for everyone to keep at the top of their minds during the conversation. This focus helps streamline discussions, ensuring that every suggested idea is a pathway toward the ultimate goal. As ideas emerge, evaluate them against this objective. For instance, a team working on a project might set *"on-time delivery within budget"* as their North Star. Ideas that most closely align with getting the project completed on time while adhering to budget and resource constraints, should clearly emerge as the top choice.

Feel free to blend these strategies to suit your group's dynamics. Perhaps the majority votes to select a leader or the North Star aids in prioritizing options before a final vote. Flexibility and a diversity of ideas can guide your team to success.

However, be mindful of falling into the trap of endless deliberations. Set a time limit to maintain momentum, guarding against the pitfalls of overthinking. One effective technique is to use a structured agenda with specific times allotted for each phase of the discussion, helping to avoid Analysis Paralysis and keep the decision-making process on track.

Tip: Employ both divergent and convergent thinking skills. During the ideation phase, encourage creativity and innovation with divergent thinking. Explore all options, employing different brainstorming techniques. Then, shift to convergent thinking to narrow down these options and select the most viable solution. Questions like *"Which of these options best achieves our goal?"* can facilitate this transition.

Navigating group decisions can be challenging, but with these strategies, you can guide your team to success. Whether you elect a leader, use majority rule, or align decisions with a North Star goal, remember that flexibility and thoughtful time management are key. By blending divergent thinking for creativity and convergent thinking for decision-making, you can keep the process focused and effective. Ultimately, the goal is to ensure that every voice is heard while driving the group toward a clear, actionable decision.

Moving Beyond Fear: Effective Decision-Making

Fear, a powerful survival instinct, can protect us from immediate danger. Yet, in high-stakes business, it can also prevent progress.

In my 20s, while hiking in Colorado with friends, we heard the telltale warning of a rattlesnake. Instinct froze me in place, my friend calmly pointed out the threat, allowing us to quickly choose a safer path. In this situation, instinct served its purpose. In business, however, fear-based decisions can keep your organization from making real progress.

Business Complexity Requires Facts

In business, success demands moving beyond fear to make data-driven decisions. Consider entering a new market: without data, fear may deem it too risky. However, market research, competitor analysis, and customer insights can transform uncertainty into a confident Go-To-Market strategy. Innovation thrives on informed risks; after all, if your data already predicts the outcome, is it really a risk?

Clarity Through Facts

Have you ever wondered why past decisions seem so obvious in hindsight? It's because the facts are clear. In uncertain moments, leverage facts to bring clarity and overcome fear-induced paralysis.

Timing in Decision-Making

You might be thinking that split-second decisions are sometimes necessary—and you'd be correct. Time can dictate how you manage a situation. In urgent scenarios, like sudden market shifts, quick instincts and experience can guide you. However, hasty decisions without sufficient data can carry significant risks. Taking a breath and assessing the situation—even in fast-paced environments—can improve outcomes.

For less urgent decisions, let time be your ally. Use it to gather facts, consult experts, and analyze trends to enable choices that mitigate risks and maximize opportunities.

A Simple Decision-Making Framework.□
Ask yourself 2 questions:

1. What's the deadline?
Weigh the need for thorough data collection against the urgency of the situation.

2. Is there immediate urgency?
Yes: Rely on experience and available data to act decisively.
No: Gather facts, analyze thoroughly, and make a fact-based decision.

Just as a rattlesnake can block your trail, fear can immobilize business decisions. By using facts as your guide in decision-making, you and your team can move forward with confidence, embracing strategic choices that drive real growth. Balancing instinct with data transforms fear into informed action, allowing your business to succeed.

Critical Thinking: An Engineer's Approach to Daily Challenges

Interested in tackling everyday problems with the efficiency of an engineer? Engineers are master problem-solvers. You don't have to be an engineer to think like one; these skills are useful throughout our daily lives. Here are some tips to help you elevate the critical thinking skills within you.

Clarify the Problem

Start with a clear understanding of the problem, which makes it easier to solve. This keeps you focused and clearly defines what success looks like for your solution. Ask yourself if you're looking at the problem or just a symptom of it. Dig deeper until you can see the underlying issue. This understanding will allow you to get to the heart of the problem.

Experience and Brainstorm

Next, look back at how you've handled similar issues in the past—drawing on your own experiences is invaluable. Brainstorming involves sharing ideas with a colleague or a friend, which can be incredibly beneficial, as two heads are often better than one. Write down as many ideas as possible, then use your initial understanding of the problem to sift through these ideas and identify the most promising solutions.

Choose an Idea

Assess your ideas with time constraints and priorities in mind. Not every situation allows for the ideal solution. For instance, if you encounter a flat tire, your options might include fixing it, using a spare, or purchasing a new tire. On the side of the road, opting for the spare is likely the best choice given the circumstances.

Fix the Problem

Implement your chosen solution. The goal is to solve the problem efficiently, using the most suitable approach. Concentrate on resolving the core issue rather than just addressing superficial symptoms.

Test Your Solution

After addressing the problem, test your solution to ensure it performs as expected. Even if you've followed the steps, be prepared to make some adjustments. Problem-solving often involves adaptation through trial and error, leading to continuous improvement.

Evaluate and Improve

Finally, assess your solution based on the test results. Use this feedback to make any necessary adjustments. Remember not to get lost in the details—take a step back to consider the bigger picture.

Practical Example

When preparing a document, research the latest information on your topic. Next, create a detailed outline tailored to your audience's needs. Start by writing down all your ideas on paper without worrying about formatting—get your thoughts out. Once your draft is complete, refine your document and seek feedback from a trusted peer. Incorporate this feedback, then give your document a final proofread before publishing.

By this point, you may realize, *"I already do this!"* By intentionally applying these steps, you can tackle almost any challenge. This method aids in finding solutions and also helps build your critical thinking skills, improving how you perceive and address problems in everyday situations.

Thought Exercise: Rethinking The Domain of Thinking

Have you come across the term non-linear thinking? It often describes people who don't follow a traditional, structured approach in their thought process. These individuals jump from idea to idea, effortlessly connecting disparate thoughts. They're often incredible problem-solvers—what you might call *"solutionists."* Having a couple of people like this on your team brings real value through their diversity of thought. However, they rarely thrive in strictly defined roles or rigid structures, which they see as challenges to overcome rather than boundaries to work within.

Let me introduce a new term: *"Omni-Domain Thinking"*. As someone who spends time thinking about thinking—a meta-thinker—I've realized that I don't prefer the term *"Non-Linear Thinker."* Instead, I prefer *"Omni-Domain Thinker."*

Omni-Domain means thinking across all domains at the same time, without being limited to any one domain at any given moment. It's about focusing on attributes and context and looking for patterns. This way of thinking helps find similarities, knowing that some things will be different, but you're focusing on similarities, not the differences.

As a mentor, I work with diverse people, and helping them find solutions is something I do often. Many seemingly complex problems are resolved simply by applying a solution from another context. Some of the patents I've worked on were simply about taking a solution from one domain and applying it to another. There wasn't anything particularly novel about the solution—it just hadn't been used in that domain before.

Omni-Domain thinking is about moving past traditional domains—you allow your mind to make connections across different areas of knowledge.

Consider this simple example: Which two are more similar—*"cat"*, *"dog"*, or *"car"*? Most people will quickly say *"cat"* and *"dog"*, yet the words *"cat"* and *"car"* share the same two starting letters *"ca."* The similarity depends entirely on the context in which you view the comparison.

To illustrate this, let's try a simple exercise. Take 60 seconds and think of as many things as you can that come to mind with the phrase: *"The Ripple Effect."*

Our minds love to categorize and group things. Because of this, many people get stuck in single-domain thinking. They can't see a solution because they're only looking at the problem from one viewpoint. It's like pushing a boulder up a hill—your perspective changes as you move from the bottom to the top. The problem doesn't change, but how you see it does.

When faced with a complex problem, shift your perspective. Ask how it might be solved in another context, and practice drawing on solutions from different domains. Omni-Domain Thinking helps connect ideas, revealing that the answer may already exist—just waiting to be applied in a new way.

Here is a fun example:

Schrödinger's cat = frozen wood frog

Navigating the Challenges of Leading a Major Project

Leading a major project is one of the most daunting challenges a tech executive can face. With millions of dollars, countless personnel hours, and the company's reputation on the line, the pressure is immense to deliver on time, on budget, and to an exceptional standard. Over my career, I've led more major initiatives than I can count, experiencing both clear successes and failures that became valuable learning experiences. Today, I want to share the straightforward recipe I've found for guiding these make-or-break projects across the finish line to outstanding results.

A seasoned Project Leader will tell you the following:

Define the Destination

Begin by understanding where you are and where you want to reach. At this stage, ignore the *"how"* and focus solely on *"what"* success looks like. This vision will serve as your guiding star, keeping you aligned and within scope despite potential doubts and obstacles.

Map Out Milestones

Once you have defined clear requirements and determined project goals, map out the significant milestones necessary for success. Setting goals and milestones helps you monitor overall project progression and keep the project on track instead of falling behind.

Maintain Discipline

Stick to your plan even when things get chaotic. Adapt and adjust as needed, but resist the temptation to add *"one more thing."* Staying within the original scope ensures that you achieve initial success, and you can always add more later.

Embrace Adaptability

Remember the old adage: *"The best-laid plans."* Between milestones, things will inevitably go wrong and get messy. Leverage your Subject Matter Experts (SMEs) and skilled Project Managers to stay on course. Adaptability and readiness to pivot are essential for success. Don't sweat the small stuff—while this phase often goes unnoticed, it's vital for reaching the next milestone, one step at a time.

Recognize When to Fail Early

If your assumptions don't hold up or your proof of concept keeps failing, it's better to call it quits early. No one wants to be the Project Leader who declares a project a failure, but it's far worse to persist with a doomed project or falsely present it as on track.

Celebrate the Wins

To motivate the team, celebrate the wins, even the small ones. Show that you value the team and they will follow you while you lead them to innovation and success.

Leading a major project is challenging, but with a clear vision, careful planning, adaptability, and discipline, you will effectively overcome these challenges. Apply these principles and see how they can transform your project management approach. With these skills, you will lead your team to success!

Playing to Win

What does it mean to be a team?

A team isn't something you simply join—it's something you become.

Think back to the playground. When you wanted to play a game, you didn't ask for resumes. It didn't matter who they were, what they believed, or where they came from. You played together because it was more fun than playing alone.

As kids, we didn't question teamwork—we just played. But somewhere along the way, that instinct faded. We started measuring, comparing, and treating teamwork as a function rather than a force. The best teams don't just work together—they are better because of each other.

Sports as a Winning Model

Now, look at your favorite professional sport. The best teams operate the same way. It's about the unspoken agreement that when the game is on, nothing matters but giving your best to help the team win.

What about individual sports like wrestling, swimming, or tennis? It may look like a solitary figure competes alone, but do they?

Does a wrestler improve alone? No. They need practice partners who push them. Does a swimmer set their best times racing an empty lane? Of course not. Their fastest swims come from the person beside them, pushing them to be just a little faster. And does a tennis player improve without someone to compete against? Never. That's why we talk about *"healthy competition"*—because the right challenger makes you better.

Take baseball: each player has a role, and the coach's job is to put the best person in each position. No one wins a baseball game alone. A team wins when every player contributes at their best.

Put Me In, Coach

A great leader, like a great coach, knows where to put people so they can thrive. But even the best strategy falls apart without commitment. Winning isn't just about having a game plan—it's about showing up for each other. Only when a team is fully engaged, working toward a shared goal, does real success happen.

Think about your own team. Who are you passing the ball to? Who is pushing you to improve? And just as important—how are you helping your teammates step up and give their best? Are you setting the example?

Playing to Win

Here's the secret: the best ideas don't come from working alone. The strongest teams aren't just a collection of individuals; they're people who challenge, support, and elevate each other. So don't just show up, keep your head down, and get by. Engage. Push yourself. Play to win. When you do, your sense of success will never be the same.

Become part of the team—because when you do, everyone wins!

The Role of Discipline in Effective Leadership

Want to get the most out of your team? It starts with you. In my career, I have observed how some leaders can inspire team performance, while others struggle, even with the same resources.

Discipline is essential for effective leadership. Yet, the word *"discipline"* often carries a negative connotation. Leadership involves setting clear expectations and consistently sticking to them, a practice that goes beyond mere words to embody a *"lead by example"* approach.

Leading by Example

To inspire your team, be a role model for discipline. Set the standard by consistently arriving on time, efficiently tackling tasks, and treating everyone respectfully. Your team will start to mirror your behavior, boosting productivity and morale. Disciplined leadership can shape a positive team culture and improve outcomes.

Providing Clear Expectations

Discipline helps leaders provide clear expectations. Without it, teams can be like players in a game without a clear set of rules — resulting in confusion and poor performance. A disciplined leader offers guidance that helps the team work well together and achieve their goals.

Keeping Projects on Track

Discipline plays a key role in keeping projects focused and on schedule, preventing them from becoming larger and more complex than planned. By sticking to set goals and deadlines, leaders help ensure projects meet their intended outcomes, which boosts efficiency and improves results. This clarity typically motivates teams through transparency and understanding.

Setting Goals for Your Team

In my role as a mentor, I once helped a leader who was managing an important project. He started by actively listening to the great ideas of his team and letting them take charge of their work. Yet, over time their work stalled, they spent too much time analyzing options without making any progress. I advised the leader to actively guide the team towards clear goals and timelines. Leaders need to manage company resources wisely and show meaningful progress. This lesson helped the leader effectively focus the team, move forward, and show real progress.

Balanced Leadership

Although it may seem counter, disciplined leadership isn't just about being rigid; it's about adaptability and choosing a clear path based on current priorities. Effectively guiding yourself and your team requires a balance of transparent goals and the flexibility to adapt. This balance is essential for achieving successful team outcomes.

Reflect on your own leadership style. Are there areas where increased discipline could enhance your effectiveness? Could your team benefit from clear expectations? Sometimes, improvement is as simple as setting a specific weekly goal and clearly explaining the plan. Remember, becoming a better leader involves continuous growth, and every disciplined step you take is a step toward a more successful team. Make those steps count.

Focus On Effective Key Metrics

Recently, I worked with an executive eager to establish key metrics for their team. Their draft, however, included 32 metrics for a single role with a high average target goal of 94%—a setup that, though well-intentioned, felt more overwhelming than motivating. With so many metrics and such high expectations, teams may lose sight of what truly drives success. Effective metrics should be clear, attainable, and provide strategic alignment between employees and company goals.

Below is the streamlined framework I provided to help this team redefine its metrics and lead them toward success:

Prioritize What Matters Most

Identify 3 to 5 critical areas that align with strategic objectives. Focusing on what matters most keeps the team centered on the priorities that drive success.

Balance the Metrics

Use a mix of financial, operational, and strategic metrics to ensure a well-rounded performance view without administrative overload.

Set Realistic, Impactful Targets

Define targets that encourage growth without setting the team up for failure:
- A target that's realistically achievable 50-60% of the time
- An 80% threshold is a good baseline for success
- A maximum stretch of 100-130% to reward exceptional performance

Communicate Clear Expectations

Connect each metric directly to organizational goals, clarifying expected outcomes so team members can understand and own their contributions.

Establish Meaningful Incentives

Create incentive structures that drive employees, eliminating complacency. Aligning rewards with individual performance will motivate the team and give them a reason to both meet and exceed their goals.

Prioritize Regular Feedback

Implement ongoing performance discussions to allow for real-time adjustments. Regular check-ins help maintain alignment with changing priorities—promoting adaptability.

Encourage Ownership

Empower team members to take charge of their metrics, promoting a culture of self-discipline, accountability, and innovation. Focusing on essential areas reduces micromanagement, enabling leaders to drive strategic impact.

This framework combines clarity and flexibility, helping leadership teams zero in on what truly drives success. Use it as a foundation to refine metrics and goals within your organization and create a clear path toward impactful results.

For more goal-setting ideas, explore the SMART Goals framework—it's versatile and effective at any level.

Thinking About Simplicity in a Complex World

Some say the world is messy and complex—nuanced, layered, and ambiguous. And while that's true to an extent, it's not always as complex as it seems. For me, there's a kind of magic in turning complexity into simplicity. It's the satisfaction of reducing life's clutter, solving a challenging problem, or crafting an effective post.

But simplicity isn't the enemy of complexity—they are companions. Think of it like sculpting a block of marble: the masterpiece emerges through deliberate effort, revealing the beauty within. Simplicity comes from understanding something deeply enough to clear away the unnecessary and uncover the clarity waiting inside.

Asking *"What If?"* and Loving the Answer

When you walk by a bookshelf, what compels you to pick up one book over another? It's a powerful human trait—curiosity.

Critical thinking begins with a curious question: *"What if I'm wrong?"* When we challenge ourselves, we open our minds to deeper understanding. Knowing is a surface-level skill useful for facts and trivia; understanding requires going beyond the surface to where everything aligns and makes sense.

Without being wrong, how would we know what was right?

And here's the thing about being wrong—it's not the failure we're taught to fear. Every mistake is a lesson, a step closer to getting it right. It's a chance to see the world from a new perspective, to ask better questions, and to uncover better answers. Isn't that what learning is all about?

Balancing Exploration and Focus

Exploration allows creativity to take shape in any direction, each idea leading to exciting possibilities. But without focus, those creative thinking *"what if"* moments can pull us off track. The key is to guide our thoughts with intention.

Focus gives creativity direction, transforming ideas into meaningful outcomes. With intentional direction, scattered ideas become deliberate progress. The discipline to evaluate and prioritize brings clarity to what matters most.

A Quiet Moment

In a world filled with noise and expectations, solitude offers the space to transform curiosity into clarity. Our minds need time for reflection, where ideas are given room to settle and take shape. These moments of quiet are less about escape and more about recalibration. They're the pause that sharpens focus and reveals what matters most.

Finding Patterns and Playfulness

Our minds are wired to recognize patterns, turning the seemingly random into something meaningful. Creativity flourishes as intellectual play when paired with curiosity. Exploring ideas with a playful mindset can lead to breakthroughs.

At the heart of it all is a paradox: to simplify, embrace complexity. To gain clarity, you must question the obvious. To stay grounded, you must allow yourself to explore. Yet, maintain balance—of continuous practice of learning and unlearning, of curiosity and focus.

An Intelligent Architecture of Mastery

In every organization, team intelligence is more than how many smart people you have; it's the diversity of thought that drives success. Intelligence is not a hierarchy; it's a system where each person adds value, like bricks in a wall, each supporting the others. Let's use that wall as a framework for this discussion.

Average Thinker: sees a challenge and tackles it head-on, using raw effort and persistence. They're the doers, the executors, the ones who move the wall by sheer willpower alone. They bring the momentum and grit, essential for driving initiatives forward. They get things done!

Smart Thinker: introduces strategy. They see the wall as a problem to be solved efficiently. They create plans, coordinate resources, and lead execution. Their intelligence is procedural, turning vision into action. They transform force into strategy, optimizing effort without losing momentum. This is where inspiration begins!

Exceptional Thinker: sees the wall not just as bricks but as a system of interdependencies. They perceive complexities others miss, crafting intricate solutions that account for every variable. Their vision is so advanced that explaining it becomes the challenge. They know it will work but struggle to articulate why. Their brilliance is both their power and their challenge. This is where innovation begins!

Master Thinker: sees the wall as it truly is—a collection of bricks that can be moved piece by piece. They understand complexity so deeply that they can break it down without losing its essence. They communicate complexity with simplicity, guiding others to see what they see. They're architects of understanding, building clarity from complexity. Simple is the answer!

In leadership, this understanding is transformative. Constructing a balanced system of thinking means placing each brick where it supports the whole. Visionaries need executors. Strategists need doers. Architects of thought need builders of action. Intelligence diversity creates a unified team.

Good leaders recognize the value each person brings. Average thinkers provide the force and perseverance needed to get things done. Smart thinkers bring strategic execution and inspiration. Exceptional thinkers drive innovation with visionary solutions. Master thinkers bridge vision and understanding, empowering others to see the bigger picture.

Great leaders recognize both talent and structure. They see the wall as a series of bricks, each one essential and valuable. When a wall needs to be moved, they know how to break it down and rebuild it somewhere new. They can also repeat their process, again and again.

Section 6

Advanced Leadership

Next-level thinking for experienced leaders

The Power of Emotional Intelligence in Leadership

When interviewing leaders, domain skills are often highly sought after. Yet, another skill worth looking out for is emotional intelligence (EI). Although it might not always be in the spotlight, mastering EI is as essential for a leader as any domain knowledge. Emotional intelligence is about understanding and managing your emotions while helping others manage their own, making it a key ingredient in effective leadership. It is like having a toolbox of emotions and knowing when to use the right one.

Removing Obstacles

Consider a common workplace scenario: an unexpected obstacle threatens to disrupt a project timeline. A leader skilled in emotional intelligence steps in. They sense the team's anxiety with empathy while using clear communication to guide everyone through the challenge. This approach doesn't just solve problems—it also fosters creativity and strengthens the team's trust in their leader.

Recognizing Potential

How does a leader know if each team member is reaching their full potential? How do they ensure each individual is positioned to not only meet but exceed expectations? How can they recognize that the quiet team member in the corner has an undiscovered potential to excel? This is where the power of emotional intelligence shines.

Resolving Conflicts

Emotional intelligence also becomes invaluable for resolving conflicts. Imagine a situation where a disagreement between two team members could have derailed a project. A leader with strong EI can step in and mediate effectively to keep discussions productive and respectful. This ensures the team stays on task and the work culture remains collaborative while maintaining value in diverse opinions.

Team Motivation

Beyond solving conflicts, emotional intelligence helps in motivating a team. Leaders who connect emotionally with their team members can better understand their needs, goals, and motivations. Leading by example, such leaders create a workplace culture that values empathy, understanding, and respect.

Value Add

By seeking out and hiring good leaders with high EI, you will enhance your team's value. Building an inclusive environment that appreciates diverse viewpoints will cultivate an innovative mindset. Remember, the path to better morale and productivity starts with empathy, understanding, and the impactful use of emotional intelligence.

The Secret Weapon: Emotional Intelligence in Leadership

If you are looking to fill a leadership role within your organization, seek out candidates who possess both domain expertise and emotional intelligence (EI). Though often overlooked, EI is a secret weapon essential for effective leadership.

What is Emotional Intelligence?

Emotional intelligence is about understanding and managing your emotions while helping others navigate their own. It's like having a toolbox of emotions and knowing when to use the right one. When an unexpected obstacle arises, a leader with high EI can sense the team's anxiety, communicate clearly, and calmly guide everyone through the challenge.

Fostering a Positive Team Dynamic

Emotional intelligence allows leaders to create a positive team dynamic by effectively navigating conflicts and understanding individual motivations. When disagreements arise, a leader with strong EI can mediate in a way that promotes healthy debate and collaboration. Moreover, emotionally intelligent leaders take the time to connect with each team member, gaining a deeper understanding of their unique needs, goals, and motivations. This understanding enables them to create a more supportive and engaging work environment that brings out the best in every individual.

A Culture of Diversity and Collaboration

Leaders skilled with high EI foster a culture of diversity and collaboration by creating psychological safety. They recognize the value of diverse perspectives and experiences unique to each team member. By actively listening, showing empathy, and promoting open communication, these leaders create an environment where everyone feels heard, respected, and supported.

Innovation

This inclusive approach improves employee retention and encourages innovative thinking. When diverse viewpoints are welcomed and celebrated, teams are more likely to generate creative solutions and adapt to challenges. Emotionally intelligent leaders understand that the path to better morale, productivity, and organizational success starts with cultivating a culture of empathy, understanding, and collaboration.

Practical Advice

To develop your EI skills:
1. Practice active listening
2. Be aware of your own emotions
3. Show empathy and understanding

Fractional Executives: Leading Tomorrow's Innovation

Innovation is about thinking outside the box and boldly challenging the status quo. Who better than a fractional executive to bring fresh ideas and ignite the spark of innovation within your organization? If everyone in the group thinks the same, are we really getting unique and diverse ideas? Innovation requires divergent thinking.

Now, let's clear up some myths: fractional leadership is not the same as consulting. Consultants get paid for their experience, insights, and expert advice, but they might not stick around to see if their ideas are put into action. Fractional leadership involves holding the title and responsibilities of an executive, fully investing in building a successful team and supporting them throughout the change process.

Imagine giving a one-hour presentation – just because it's short doesn't mean you don't give it your all. Some people might only know you for that hour, so you must bring your best. Taking time off or working part-time doesn't make you less committed; fractional leaders are all about being fully invested and giving their best, no matter the timeframe. It's like bringing in super powered talent while making it simple and affordable for the company's bottom line.

My ask is for you to embrace Fractional Executives in practical roles, leading you to be the innovators of tomorrow. Bring in a unique perspective that sparks a revolution for change. Remember, embracing diversity brings about a diversity of thought – a key ingredient for success.

A Silent Revolution: Embracing Fractional Leadership

Have you noticed the subtle yet transformative shift in executive leadership? In today's fast-paced business world, driven by progress and innovation, a quiet revolution is reshaping how we lead—one that emphasizes diversity and collaboration.

At the core of this change is the *"fractional executive"*—an innovative concept empowering businesses to access shared resources and deep expertise, guiding companies toward a more inclusive and flexible leadership approach.

Fractional leadership prompts a departure from the traditional top-down model towards *"collaborative leadership."* Here, leadership becomes a catalyst for innovation, recognizing the potential in others, staying open to learning, and understanding that leadership is about asking the right questions instead of having all the answers.

The importance of humility in today's leadership is clear. Being a fractional executive requires setting aside ego and fostering a culture where each team member's contribution is valued, and every voice is heard.

Leverage fractional executives whose principles are rooted in humility and openness. Actively embrace this inclusive leadership style, paving the way for collaborative and productive teams. Empathy and a willingness to receive feedback enable fractional executives to quickly create an environment where trust is foundational, strengthening team dynamics, and mentoring your leadership team on strategic decision-making.

Standing on the edge of this silent revolution, the call to embrace humility and inclusivity in leadership is evident. Navigating the complexities of the modern business world requires continuous adaptability and openness. The future of collaborative leadership is here. Let's lead with humility, leverage fractional executives, and pave the way for a world where every individual's potential is fully realized.

The Power of Fraction: Diverse Perspectives, Humility, and Inclusivity

In today's fast-paced business world, where decisions carry significant weight and can have lasting consequences for organizations, effective leadership is indispensable. It involves putting aside ego and embracing diverse viewpoints. Fractional leadership relies on this humility while leveraging diverse perspectives to make well-informed decisions.

Fostering a culture of openness and humility involves practical actions like encouraging open conversations, leading by example, admitting mistakes, seeking diverse opinions, and evaluating decision-making processes. This is particularly important in the tech sector, where innovation moves quickly, and understanding opportunities and their potential impact is essential.

Recognizing and addressing personal biases is more than just a good trait—it's a catalyst for collaboration. Encouraging an environment where every voice, regardless of origin, is valued and welcomed brings true diversity.

By embracing humility and inclusivity, fractional executives continuously fuel innovation, creating an atmosphere where growth and success become shared achievements. Fractional executives, adept at managing investments and resources, create an environment driven by innovation.

In summary, many Fractional Executives have the skills to secure full-time high-paying jobs with top companies. However, they choose to offer their expertise at a fractional rate to support organizations that may not afford them otherwise. Their willingness to assist companies in need is admirable, allowing them to continuously enhance their skills at a pace seldom seen in traditional settings.

The Ripple Effect: The Profound Impact of Effective Leadership

Effective leadership is more than just a skill; it's a rare quality that holds the power to shape entire societies. Like a rare gem, top leaders are prized for their unique ability to provide clarity and vision within an organization. Yet, their significance extends far beyond strategic vision, reaching into the very fabric of our communities and collective well-being.

Top leaders, with their ability to attract and retain top talent, prioritize the growth and well-being of their team members and create an environment where employees feel valued, inspired, and empowered to realize their full potential. This promotes loyalty and retention while nurturing a culture of innovation, resilience, and excellence. By fostering emotional intelligence, trust, and the ability to remove obstacles, these leaders establish a workplace where individuals thrive professionally and personally.

Moreover, good leadership transcends beyond the office, influencing entire societies. By promoting a healthy work-life balance and emphasizing the importance of self-care and family, leaders contribute to the well-being of individuals beyond office walls. This holistic approach to leadership fosters a community of healthy, energized individuals who bring their best selves to work and home, celebrating diversity and embracing resilience in all its forms.

Effective leaders are often great communicators, actively listening to their team members' ideas and concerns. This fosters a culture of openness and collaboration, where diversity is celebrated. Such inclusive environments create teams that excel at problem-solving, divergent thinking, and driving solutions. Imagine a society where these skills become the norm—a society built on true diversity and collaboration where healthy debates inspire minds instead of leading to violence.

This ripple effect of effective leadership can be profound and transformative, shaping the very essence of our communities. It inspires individuals to reach new heights of personal and professional fulfillment. I urge you, when you discover such leaders within your organization, to appreciate and recognize their value and do everything within your power to retain their contributions. Through acts of integrity, empathy, and vision, these leaders drive organizational success and light the way for a brighter, more compassionate future for us all.

Bias in AI: Truth, Fact, and Human Perception

The human world is full of bias.

Unconscious bias: occurs when hidden attitudes influence our decisions, often shaped by our upbringing or experiences.

Implicit bias: involves unconscious attitudes affecting our actions, even if we consciously reject stereotypes.

Artificial Intelligence (AI) is a tool that relies on the availability of large amounts of data for the models to learn effectively. Every day, humans generate massive amounts of data unintentionally filled with biases, feeding these AI algorithms.

While AI cannot be biased, the algorithms learn from information that is often biased, leading to biased conclusions. Achieving 100% bias-free data for AI is a challenge, but is it the solution? Would this data be cold and accurate? Would it be relatable or make sense to humans living in a world full of bias?

Confirmation bias: happens when a single source or insufficient amount of data guides our conclusions or beliefs.

AI algorithms will also be influenced by the variety of data. If the dataset is limited or comes from a single source, the output from AI may appear biased. This means that the source of truth for an AI model will be reflective of the data it was given.

Truth: A belief accepted as true, reflecting a subjective perspective or acceptance.

Fact: Information proven to be true, indicating a more objective and verifiable reality.

If enough people collectively believe something to be true, does it become *"truth?"* When most people believed that the world was flat instead of round, did that make it true? It certainly didn't make it fact, but did this human belief make this notion the truth? Humans often define their own truths based on what they believe.

Differentiating between truth and fact is vital when navigating discussions about AI biases. Humans have beliefs based on information they know to be true, and an AI model's source of truth is determined by the data we provide.

Summary: AI cannot be inherently biased. However, the data fed into the models may give the appearance of bias based on learning from human-created data. This highlights the pivotal role of humans in the process. Humans have the advantage here because we can become aware of our biases and actively work to manage them. If we want our AI's to appear less biased, it starts with us providing a more accurate and unbiased source for AI models to learn from.

Unlocking AI's Potential Through Contextual Memory

AI tools offer remarkable efficiency, yet one limitation remains—contextual memory. Many AI tools rely on a token-based memory window, meaning the more verbose an interaction becomes, the less active memory is available. For instance, *"Hello"* is a single token, and *"How are you today?"* requires four. Concise language is the key to keeping more information within an AI's memory.

However, any limitation brings room for improvement. By advancing how AI stores, retrieves and learns from interactions, we can build more adaptive systems.

Contextual vs Token-Based Memory

The key lies in applying AI's natural language processing to contextual memory. Instead of processing *"Hello"* and *"How are you today?"* as separate tokens, they could be condensed into a single token like *"Hi."* This significantly increases memory efficiency compared to a token-based approach.

Attribute Framework

An attribute-based framework enables AI to store key information and update it dynamically. This reduces memory usage while retaining key details.

Example:
Verbatim (37 tokens):
Joe is an accomplished author known for weaving complex themes into engaging narratives, often exploring the intersection of technology and human creativity. His writing is celebrated for its sophisticated style and profound insights into the human condition.

Attributes (12 tokens):
Name: Joe
Role: Author
Style: Sophisticated, thought-provoking
Themes: Technology, creativity, human condition

By storing memory data similar to how humans process information, memory becomes more efficient and adaptive as new details emerge.

Comprehension vs Understanding

Comprehension involves receiving meaningful information, whereas understanding means making sense of it. Improved contextual memory allows AI to offer more meaningful responses tailored to the user.

Memory Recall

For verbatim recall, AI can store data as document artifacts, similar to how search engines work. Alternatively, the AI system could prompt users with, *"Please remind me of that document,"* avoiding unnecessary assumptions or guesses.

Pattern Recognition

Using attribute-based memory, AI could recognize patterns across domains, helping to find metaphors or similarities outside specific areas of knowledge. This versatility would aid comprehension across a broader range of topics.

User Profiling

AI could use attributes across sessions to tailor interactions. Profiling based on language choices could enhance responses, accounting for education level, culture, or location. All data can remain anonymized to ensure privacy.

A Path Forward

AI's next leap may not come from hardware upgrades or larger datasets, but from refining contextual memory. By mimicking human memory's adaptive nature, we can create AI systems that do more than generate text—they improve human-AI interactions.

About the author

I am a fractional CTO and technology leader with 30+ years of experience helping organizations align technology strategy with business goals. I specialize in developing authentic leadership, building psychological safety within teams, and simplifying complexity to drive measurable outcomes.

I began writing on LinkedIn in early 2024, publishing over 100 posts in 18 months. My writing focuses on servant leadership, team self-sufficiency, and the human side of technology leadership. Through my blog posts, I share insights on transforming directive management into collaborative leadership that empowers teams to excel independently.

As a technology leader, executive coach, advisor, and board member, I bring deep expertise in enterprise architecture, SaaS transformations, and global team leadership. I believe startup companies should have the same access to strategic leadership as Fortune 100 companies—which drives my fractional CTO practice helping high-growth organizations scale effectively.

I've presented at 30+ conferences and podcasts, coached leaders from startup founders to Fortune 100 executives, and served as a strategic advisor.